CONTEMPORARY MIND
SOME MODERN ANSWERS

By J. W. N. Sullivan

Copyright © 2019 Read & Co. Science

This edition is published by Read & Co. Science,
an imprint of Read Books Ltd.

This book is copyright and may not be reproduced or copied in any way without the express permission of the publisher in writing.

British Library Cataloguing-in-Publication Data
A catalogue record for this book is available from the British Library.

www.readandcobooks.co.uk

J. W. N. Sullivan

John William Navin Sullivan was a popular writer on science and literature, author of a celebrated study on Beethoven. He wrote one of the earliest accounts of Einstein's *General Theory of Relativity* and circulated amongst the literary elite of London, including Aldous Huxley, Wyndham Lewis and T.S. Eliot. Sullivan's early days are somewhat murky however. He was known to frequently lie about his upbringing, telling Aldous Huxley that he was born in Ireland and attended *Maynooth* with James Joyce. In fact, he was born on 22 January 1886 in the East End of London, England, and worked at a Telegraph company from 1900 onwards. The directors of the firm recognised his outstanding mathematical capabilities, and financed Sullivan's study at the *Northern Polytechnic Institute*. From 1908 to 1910, Sullivan studied and researched at *University College London*, but left without a degree and moved to America, where he became a journalist. Sullivan's peripatetic life continued, and in 1913 he returned to Britain, still employed as a journalist, before working for the ambulance service in Serbia during the First World War. After the war, Sullivan wrote for *The New Witness* and *The Athenaeum*. He married his first wife, Sylvia Mannooch in 1917 and they had one daughter, Navina, born in November 1921. It was at *The Athenaeum,* one of the best known and important literary reviews of the 1920s that Sullivan was introduced to the London literary world. He continued contributing literary and scientific articles to *The Athenaeum* well into the 1920s, but also wrote for the *Times Literary Supplement, The Adelphi* and *John O'London's Weekly*. During this time, Sullivan wrote his explanation of Einstein's theory of relativity, as well as numerous articles noting the new spirit of creativity in the sciences and the possibility of their reconciliation with the arts. These articles were collated in *Aspects of Science* in 1923. Sullivan went on to pen the well-received study, *Beethoven: His Spiritual Development* (1927) and contributed to *An Outline of Modern Knowledge* (1931). Sullivan separated from his first wife in 1921, and married Vere Bartrick Baker in 1928, with whom he had a son, Navin. In the early 1930s, Sullivan was increasingly troubled by poor health however, and was diagnosed in 1934 as suffering from *disseminated sclerosis*, a form of creeping paralysis. He died on 11 August, 1937 in Chobham, Surrey.

PREFACE

SOME little time ago I had the good fortune to interview a number of the leading representatives of thought in this country, France, and Germany. My object was to elicit the opinions of these men on certain fundamental questions. The answers are reprinted in this volume. Most of these men are, naturally enough, men of science, for it is chiefly to science that we look for light and leading now-a-days.

Besides the interviews, but connected with them, are chapters dealing more fully with the questions discussed, or else illustrating certain of their implications. These implications refer chiefly to the relations between mysticism, art, and science, a matter which seems to me of the greatest importance for the new outlook towards which we are working. The dissertations on Beethoven, Maxwell, and Newton, are introduced for their bearing on this subject. The chapter on *Mathematics and Culture* was originally delivered as the Presidential Address to the London Mathematical Association, and to this its colloquial form is due.

CONTENTS

	Page
INTRODUCTION	9
THE BALANCED LIFE	19
THE PROBLEM OF SUFFERING	26
THE NECESSITY OF MYSTICISM	36
HUMAN IMMORTALITY	40
A DISSERTATION ON BEETHOVEN	50
THE SCIENTIFIC OUTLOOK	59
A DISSERTATION ON MAXWELL	65
NEW PRINCIPLES	74
A DISSERTATION ON NEWTON	78
SCIENCE AND ART	93
MATHEMATICS AND CULTURE	98
SIR JOSIAH STAMP	118
SIR A. S. EDDINGTON	124
SIR J. H. JEANS	130
M. PAINLEVÉ	137
MR. ALDOUS HUXLEY	141
PROFESSOR MAX PLANCK	148
PROFESSOR SCHRÖDINGER	154
PRINCE DE BROGLIE	160
PROFESSOR LEVY	165
MR. H. G. WELLS	172
ON PROGRESS	179

INTRODUCTION

THE problems discussed in this book may justly be called fundamental problems. They are the questions that remain, as it were, "behind" all our specialised interests. Our general outlook on life is determined chiefly by our attitude towards these questions. They have probably been discussed ever since man found sufficient leisure to think about anything other than his bodily wants. They have assumed different forms at different times, however, and the relative gravity and acuteness of them has changed considerably.

The differences between the modern age and any preceding age, so far as they are essential, are due chiefly to science. This is obviously true, of course, so far as the mere mechanism of life is concerned, but it is also true that our general outlook on life has been largely influenced by science. It is not that science has originated new answers concerning the why, whence and whither of existence, but it has made certain answers much more plausible than others.

The theory, for instance, that all life is purposeless, the product of a blind, impersonal fate, was held by Democritus and was doubtless held before him. But, in the form in which it was preached by Democritus and popularized by Lucretius, it was more the expression of an emotion than a reasoned philosophy. To say that everything came about in a purposeless manner, when no description of the process could be given, was not particularly convincing. For the world, particularly the world of animate nature, appears to be full of instances of purpose and design. But modern science has made the general outlook of Democritus much more plausible. Darwin, in his theory of natural selection, attempted to give a mechanism whereby all the exquisite adaptations we meet with in animate nature could have come about "accidentally." He stated that variations are constantly occurring in all living creatures, that some of these variations are inheritable, and that those that enable the creature to adapt itself more perfectly to its environment will tend to be preserved in the struggle for existence. In the form in which the theory was popularized by the materialists of the nineteenth century it was assumed that the variations occurred "at random." That is to say, that although the variations doubtless occur in accordance with laws of nature of which we at present know practically nothing, we are not to suppose that they reveal any purpose, any "upward and on" tendency in nature. The march from the amœba to man has not been designed. So far as the nature of things is concerned, as it were, it might have been the other way round.

Thus we see, in this particular instance, that modern science has made an age-old philosophy much more plausible. It is now possible to believe that existence is purposeless in a way quite impossible to an intelligent mediaevalist, or even to a man of Paley's time. The instances of design on which they relied have now been accounted for in terms of a purely mindless mechanism.

To say this is perhaps to go too far. The mechanism by which new adaptations are produced is not yet understood, and there are some biologists who doubt

INTRODUCTION

whether they can be accounted for by blind mechanical forces. They think that "inherent tendencies" and the like, processes not reducible to the laws of physics and chemistry, may have to be assumed in order to explain the origin and development of living things. But even if such notions are introduced it is evident that the old conception of Design, and of a Great Designer, will have been profoundly modified. For the design is carried through with a wastefulness altogether beyond human standards. For every living creature that succeeds in getting a footing in life there are thousands or millions that perish. There is an enormous random scattering for every seed that comes to life. This does not remind us of intelligent human design. "If a man, in order to shoot a hare, were to discharge thousands of guns on a great moor in all possible directions; if, in order to get into a locked-up room, he were to buy ten thousand casual keys, and try them all; if, in order to have a house, he were to build a town, and leave all the other houses to wind and weather—assuredly no one would call such proceedings purposeful, and still less would anyone conjecture behind these proceedings a higher wisdom, unrevealed reasons, and superior prudence."*

Nevertheless, the wastefulness of the process does not disprove the existence of design. We can only say that the design is carried out in a very singular manner, judged by human standards. It is an argument against the Great Designer of Christian theology, wholly benevolent, omniscient and omnipotent, but not, perhaps, against a Designer of limited power dealing with extremely intractable material. On the whole, we may

---

* Lange, "History of Materialism."

conclude that the biological theory of evolution makes the old doctrine of a purposeless universe distinctly more plausible.

Another of the great fundamental problems, the problem of suffering, is a question concerning which science seems to have nothing to say. Such increased intensity and acuteness as the problem may have acquired may be referred to the greater sensibility, on the part of the mass of the people, that has come about in modern times, and this greater sensibility has only very indirectly been influenced by scientific advances. No problem in the history of mankind has proved more insoluble than the problem of evil.

The survival of bodily death is another of the age-old questions with which we are concerned, and to this question we may definitely say that science has made a contribution. But its contribution is ambiguous. On the one hand modern physiology has made the independent existence of the mind, apart from the body, distinctly less plausible than it was before. On the other hand psychical research, which may be classed as a very rudimentary and imperfect branch of science, has produced a certain amount of evidence for the independent existence of the mind. Evidence of this kind is entirely modern. In fact, the whole psychical research movement can be dated from 1847, when the Fox sisters started their "rappings." These phenomena, if we are to believe the late confessions of the sisters themselves, were fraudulent, and the subsequent development of the movement has certainly been attended by an immense amount of fraud. It is difficult, however, to dismiss all the diverse phenomena lumped together under the name of "spiritualism" as fraudulent. But

INTRODUCTION

the best attested phenomena, such as telepathy, clairvoyance, etc., do not necessitate the hypothesis of a discarnate mind although, if we admit them, they certainly require us to oppose that there exist mental powers not taken into account by ordinary psychology. Even some of the material phenomena, such as "levitation" are difficult to explain away. In the best attested cases we can only maintain the purely "natural" explanation either by supposing that the medium was an almost unbelievably clever trickster, or else by supposing that the observers were almost unbelievably imbecile.

It is much easier to dismiss the evidence for discarnate minds, especially if we admit the existence of the extraordinary mental powers postulated by the phenomena of telepathy and clairvoyance. For it is then possible to construct hypotheses which will explain many, if not all, alleged "spirit communications" without invoking either discarnate minds or sheer fraud. It is possible, nevertheless, that there remains a modicum of phenomena which cannot be explained in this way. Dr. Broad, who has investigated these phenomena very carefully, does not believe that even these require us to assume discarnate minds and he presents us, as a *minimum* hypothesis, with his rather horrible theory of a "psychic factor," something which is not itself a mind, but which can survive physical death and, in con-function with a living physical brain, form a temporary mind.

If the evidence of psychic research leaves survival doubtful, the evidence of physiology makes it still more doubtful. For we now realise how much closer even than has generally been assumed by common sense is the relation between mind and body. A man's character, as well as his intellect, seems to be almost entirely at the mercy of his bodily functions. A benevolent saint can, it appears, be turned into a homicidal lunatic by a bodily operation. The man's "true" character, which flourishes independently of his ductless glands, seems to be a myth. As the observed correlations between bodily changes and mental changes become more numerous, it becomes more difficult to believe in the existence of a mind independent of the body. Partial destruction of the body certainly seems to involve partial destruction of the mind. It is natural to conclude that the total destruction of the one involves the total destruction of the other. But it would be very rash to take this conclusion as proved. The established correlations between bodily states and mental states are still comparatively few in number. And even were the correlations made much more numerous it might still be possible to maintain that the mind is an independent entity using the body as its instrument. On the whole, however, the theory that the mind is wholly dependent on the body, and is destroyed with it, has been made somewhat more plausible by the advances in physiology.

Even if we believe that we live in a purposeless universe and that bodily death means total annihilation it is still true that happiness is a good thing and suffering a bad one. A man who believes that the whole human adventure is purposeless may still be ardently concerned with the welfare of the human race. He may be profoundly interested in the future and wholesouled in his endeavours to make that future better than the present. The fact that he believes the emergence of

INTRODUCTION

conscious thinking beings to be a meaningless episode between two eternities need not affect his practical activities or his motives for them. For many of our activities are entirely independent of our philosophy. They do not require to be rationalized; they are their own obvious justification. All the obvious cases of "doing good to others" fall into this class. It is only when we are not quite sure where the good lies that our philosophy has any bearings on the matter. Thus those who believe that the meaning of the present is to be found in the future, that we exist to make the world better for coming generations, are not disturbed by the theoretical purposelessness of the whole human adventure. The fact that science preaches the ultimate physical death of the universe does not alter their conviction that there ought to be as much happiness as possible in the meantime.

Nevertheless there are, and always have been, many people who have a strong desire to believe that the human adventure is not ultimately purposeless, however little influence this belief may have on their actions. They find it impossible to believe that the universe is so irrational an affair as it would appear to be on the "purposeless" theory. And some of them even claim to have an intuition that it is not so. These impulses have, of course, played a large part in framing religious systems and also many of the systems of philosophy. Such systems do not impose themselves; they do not "command assent." There is no general agreement as to their validity. But these intuitions seem to have been shared by some of the greatest men that the race has produced, and it is possible to suppose, therefore, that they lie in the line of advance of the developing human consciousness. The most advanced forms of these intuitions are to be found in mysticism, and the mystical solution, when various solutions are investigated, seems to be the only really satisfactory alternative to the theory of a purposeless universe. It is from this point of view that mysticism is discussed in this book.

It is a commonplace to say that science is becoming more and more philosophical. This remark is somewhat misleading, for the scientific outlook has always, of course, presupposed a philosophy. But it is true that scientific men are becoming more conscious of the philosophy they assume. If we are to judge by the interviews contained in this book we see that the mathematical physicists, at any rate, are inclined to a form of philosophical idealism. They regard consciousness as fundamental; everything else is to be derived from it. Perhaps too much importance should not be attached to this fact. Scientific men are not usually profound students of philosophy, and it may be that they have accepted a philosophic outlook without being fully aware of what can be said for and against it. Still, the fact is significant, and suggests that a thorough investigation of the philosophic aspects of modern science is urgently required. In any case, it seems perfectly clear that a return to the naive materialism of the nineteenth century is impossible.

The contribution of modern scientific theory to the old problem of determinism versus freewill is more direct. Heisenberg's principle of Indeterminacy states that sufficient knowledge for accurate prediction can never be obtained about the ultimate constituents of matter—electrons. In order to predict the future motion of an electron, for instance, we require to know

INTRODUCTION

both its present position and its present velocity. Our measurements of these quantities are attended by a certain necessary minimum margin of error. This is not due to any theoretically remediable defects in our measuring apparatus, but is due to the fact that a certain necessary minimum interchange of energy (a quantum) is involved in our observation of the electron, and this interchange of energy is sufficient to disturb the electron in an unpredictable way. It is suggested, in particular by Professor Eddington, that since the notion of determinism, as applied to the fundamental processes of nature, is unverifiable and useless, it should be dropped. The apparently determined behaviour of the bodies ordinarily dealt with in scientific practice and daily experience is a purely statistical result. It is an average behaviour, due to the fact that the individual notions of the electrons constituting the body cancel out, as it were. And Professor Eddington suggests that this principle of indeterminacy is of great importance for the problem of freewill, if only for the reason that we are not likely to suppose that the mind is more mechanistic than an electron. It is indeed probable that the prejudice in favour of mental determinism, so largely encouraged by the apparently successful adoption of material determinism in physical science, will not persist if it turns out that science has no longer any need of the notion.

THE BALANCED LIFE

"Man is born free," said Rousseau, "and is everywhere in chains."

It is difficult to discover any interpretation of this remark which would make it sound true. Rousseau seems to have had in mind some mythological Golden Age in which naked and noble savages walked freely about the earth. There is no evidence for such an age. The evidence we have goes to show that savages are almost as cramped and limited by laws and conventions as is a modern civilized man, and in some cases the laws and conventions are even sillier than our own. If Rousseau believed that man had ever been more free than he was in eighteenth-century France, he was probably mistaken. The chains have always existed, and always will exist. Perfect individual freedom, as long as man is a member of society, is, of course, impossible.

But perhaps all that Rousseau meant was that there was once a Golden Age, before the world was cursed with civilization, when men followed their natural impulses more freely. Freedom to do whatever you want to do is probably what Rousseau meant by freedom. But there have been men to whom their natural impulses were "chains." "Oh, that I were delivered from the body of this death!" said St. Paul. To St. Paul it must have appeared that to be a human being, with all a human being's normal impulses and desires, was to be a slave. The freedom he craved for was a freedom that could only be attained by mastering the imperative urge of the bodily appetites. The elements which dominate most men's lives: hunger, sex, the desire for power and for the esteem of one's fellows, were felt by him to be constraints. The insistence of their demands was to him intolerable. To yield to them would have been for St. Paul a denial of life. The first condition of life, for him, therefore, was to be free from "the body of this death." His aim, in his endeavour to master his "natural" impulses, was not nullity, but the achievement of a more abundant life. He believed that there were elements of his being, apart from those connected with the body of this death, whose fulfilment would lead to this more abundant life. But the body is the enemy of these other impulses; only by transcending the body can they come to fruition. This idea has been shared by all the great ascetics. Only through the crucifixion of the body can man attain real freedom.

Is there any justification for this belief? Is it true that our impulses differ in value and that our "human nature" is an obstacle, hindering us in the realization of a higher, more abundant life? There have always been men who believed this, but the majority of men to-day, and doubtless in all ages, have emphatically striven after the freedom of Rousseau, and not at all after that of St. Paul. But they have, for the most part, respected the Pauline ideal. They have not coveted his freedom, but they have agreed that it is "beyond" them. The great saints, ascetics, mystics, have, on the whole, been regarded as the spiritual aristocrats of the race.

It is a testimony to the amazing degree of democracy we have now achieved that this attitude has almost entirely disappeared. Walt Whitman was the first great modern voice to preach what Santayana calls "the democracy of the passions," and the discovery is now acclaimed on every hand. An increasing body of opinion holds that every impulse is, intrinsically, as much entitled to satisfaction as any other. There is no hierarchy of the passions, as St. Paul believed. The Christian Doctrine of original sin is a myth. None of our impulses are intrinsically bad. The art of life consists in effecting a balance between our impulses and in gratifying as many of them as possible. The suppression of certain impulses in favour of others leads, on this view, to an impoverishment of life. The one sin is unbalanced excess, and it matters not what we choose to be excessive in. A man like Henry Cavendish, with his cold and exclusive passion for scientific knowledge, is, judged by this new criterion, as far removed from what a man should be as is a dipsomaniac. A man or woman obsessed with sex arouses, rightly, a certain feeling of distaste. We must learn to cultivate a similar reaction in the presence of a mathematician. Both types are excessive, and therefore imperfect. The imperfection comes, not from the fact that one appetite is abnormally developed, but from the fact that its indulgence inhibits or prevents the indulgence of other appetites. Abstinence is the real crime. Thus, if a man were abnormally sensual *and* abnormally ascetic, abnormally selfish *and* abnormally unselfish, there would be nothing to object to. He would, in fact, have life, and life more abundantly than other people. The essential thing is that his different impulses should be properly balanced. Nero was imperfect and so was Newton. But a Newton and a Nero rolled into one would probably be magnificent.

It is difficult to discover in what consists the perfect state of balance recommended by this theory. It is obvious that certain impulses are stronger in some men than in others. Indeed, certain impulses seem to be practically non-existent in some men. To say, for instance, that Newton devoted insufficient time and energy to wine, women and song, is probably to blame Newton for not indulging impulses he never possessed. For all we know, Newton never abstained from anything he wanted to do. Only he never wanted to do what most men want to do. If, therefore, we are to cry, "Poor brutes!" with Mr. Aldous Huxley, "at the sight of such extraordinary and lamentable souls as those of Kant, of Newton, of Descartes," it can hardly be on the ground that these men did not effect a balance between their impulses, but rather on the ground that certain impulses were insufficiently strong. This, surely, is a rather arbitrary objection. If a life impresses us as an harmonious and satisfactory whole, does it matter that it lacks certain elements? Is a string quartet to be condemned because it is not a full orchestra?

An apparent obscurity and incoherence in this democratic theory of the passions becomes more obvious when we meditate on the difference between Newton and an ape. Newton, that lamentable soul, so strikingly deficient in natural impulses, was probably even more removed from the ideal Rabelaisian standard than a full-blooded gorilla. Reckoned numerically, the gorilla is probably more richly endowed than Newton with impulses. And yet Newton is generally regarded as an improvement on the gorilla. In fact, our feeling that the evolutionary process has been a progress from the lower to the higher is inexplicable on this theory. When a distinctively human passion emerged, such as that passion for knowledge so excessively exemplified by Newton, man's advance in the scale of being was not simply due to the fact that he had added one to his already numerous impulses. It was not merely one step upward and on, as we must assume occurred when he developed a craving for tobacco. The difference between the animal and man is not to be explained by saying that man has a larger number of impulses, or that he effects a better balance (he probably does not) between the impulses he possesses. We must admit that some impulses are "higher" than others. It is not true that all impulses are of equal value.

In order to account satisfactorily for our conviction that some impulses are more valuable than others, it is probable that we should have to accept the philosophic doctrine of "absolute values." We would then have to suppose that what we call an advance is an increasing approximation towards the complete embodiment of these absolute values.

If we admit that there are activities which are good in themselves, then we can hardly deny that a life devoted to such activities is a good life. If knowledge is a good in itself, and not only because of its usefulness, then a life devoted to the acquisition of knowledge is a good life. It is along these lines that Newton must be justified. He was not some tropical jungle of impulses, it is true. Probably he had not even the normal dosage of "human nature." But the sort of excellence he achieved was made possible by his very limitations. Mankind definitely attained a higher level of development, in him, in a certain direction, and this direction is admirable and desirable. Man's awareness, his degree of consciousness, has been increased through the life-work of Newton. If human beings, as a whole, can be said to be up to anything, and do not exist merely in order to breed more millions of human beings, then we may be confident that Newton has helped us a step towards the goal. He has taken us further in one particular direction. If we regard the human consciousness as a developing thing, then we must surely value whatever helps forward this development. Consciousness, of course, contains many elements; every human impulse enters into it. Newton's advance is concerned with comparatively few of those elements. A more comprehensive advance, including more elements, has probably been effected by certain great artists and religious teachers. But we invariably find that the syntheses achieved by such men lay more stress on some impulses than on others. There is no reason whatever to believe that the ideal synthesis would present all impulses as of equal value. Indeed, it seems to be a necessary condition of advance that certain impulses should be subordinated.

We may, therefore, sympathise with St. Paul's desire to be free from the body of this death, even if we think he was mistaken. He was aware of elements within himself that he estimated more highly than his bodily passions—and we cannot say that he was wrong in doing so. We do not know enough about the final synthesis, or state of consciousness, that St. Paul achieved. He may have been in the line of evolution, for all we know. It may be that man will have to burn with St. Paul's fever before he reaches his goal. We feel that St. Paul was a great man, and not merely a freak. And his passion has been shared by too many illustrious examples for us to be able to dismiss it with any confidence. It is possible, even, that some of the great ascetics were not altogether unjustified in their lives, although here the freakish element certainly seems to be much more perceptible. Such men are not examples for the human race, but it may be that they were explorers and found some treasure. To assume that man already is all that he ever will be is surely unjustified. Before certain manifestations—experiments, we might call them—we must suspend judgment.

At the back of our conviction that there are higher and lower elements in our nature lies the assumption that life has a purpose, that the universe is not meaningless. The doctrine that all our impulses are of equal value does not, as its upholders assert, lead to a fuller, more varied and more intense life but, in general, to despondency and boredom. A life that serves no purpose, where there is no subordination to some final aim, is felt to be a dreary affair, for all its activities, however numerous and intense, are essentially meaningless. A man craves for his life to have direction, and no direction is possible without the subordination of some impulses to others. The unescapable boredom that affects our rich pleasure-seekers, who are, one would suppose, in the best possible position for cultivating all their impulses, is due precisely to the fact that their lives lack direction. The direction that a life assumes is determined, of course, by a man's dominant impulses. A life where every impulse was given equal weight would be entirely lacking in direction. Most men have no very strong intellectual or spiritual passions, and the direction of their lives is determined almost wholly by sex, paternity, and the herd instinct.

THE PROBLEM OF SUFFERING

The question of whether life has a meaning requires a little definition. The question is, I believe, one that everybody understands; it corresponds to a universal human wonder and anxiety. But it is possible, when one thinks about it, to find it ambiguous. This is often the case where fundamental questions are involved, and too much importance should not be attached to that fact. In particular, one should not fall into the error of supposing that the difficulty of defining something affects the existence of that thing. Most of the things that matter most to us are those which are the hardest to define. But the word "meaning" is certainly somewhat ambiguous. It has, as a matter of fact, a great wealth of meanings. A symbol, for instance, has meaning; it means what it symbolises. Also, an element in a scheme has meaning; its meaning is found in its connections with the other elements in the scheme. It is in this last sense, I think, that we ask whether life has a meaning. But even then the question admits of two interpretations. It is usual, I think, to imagine vaguely some future state of illumination which shall throw a retrospective light upon our present experience, justifying it and showing it to be wholly necessary and good. In that day, in St. Paul's words, we shall know even as we are known. Evil will be seen as "apparent"—as an aspect of good. All the pain and suffering of the world will be resolved and accounted for as indispensable elements in the great universal harmony. But there are mystics who claim that life does not need justification as an element in some all-inclusive scheme. Our experience, they assert, is justified here and now. There is nothing that has to be argued away or explained in the light of later knowledge. In the light of the mystic vision there is no problem; all is good and all is one. This way of resolving the question, if one could accept it, would seem to be the most satisfactory. Unfortunately, however, the mystic vision appears to be incommunicable.

It is, of course, the existence of evil which makes acute the question of whether life has a meaning, and which also seems to make the question insoluble. All attempts to represent life as part of a divine plan, conceived by a beneficent creator, seem to break down over the fact of suffering. These attempts usually take the form of trying to show that suffering is not evil, but an aspect of good. Good, we are told, could not exist without suffering. Suffering supplies the necessary discipline for the development of the free soul. Thus, courage cannot exist without danger, unselfishness cannot exist without sacrifice. It is true that some forms of suffering seem to enrich and perfect a life. It is also true that suffering has probably been essential to the creation of the greatest works of art we know. But there are forms of suffering for which this explanation loses all plausibility. This is particularly obvious in the case of the sufferings of children. It is also sufficiently obvious in various cases of accident and disease. A detailed description of certain episodes in human history, such as witch-burning, is also sufficient to make incredible the idea that suffering is disciplinary. One feels, indeed, that the idea is not only incredible, but contemptible. One suspects its authors of a smugness, a lack of imaginative sympathy, a cold selfishness, which is almost sub-human. At the best one can only suppose that they are so incapable of experience that they can construct their theories in a sort of imbecile detachment.

Very few men have had the courage fully to face this problem, and perhaps the greatest of these is Dostoevsky. The last word on this question, it seems to me, has been said in his chapter *Pro and Contra* in *The Brothers Karamazov*. He there gives cases, not imagined, but taken from the Russian newspapers, of sufferings inflicted on children, and on these cases he founds his argument. Many discussions on this question, as I have said, do little but reveal the insensitiveness of their authors. The theoretic, philosophic, scholarly type so often seems to lack the imagination necessary to *realize* the problem involved. The realization can only be effected through feeling, and in his capacity to awaken this feeling Dostoevsky is unique. For that reason I cannot do better than state the problem in his terms. A more abstract treatment of the problem would be an evasion of it.

Ivan Karamazov is talking to his brother Alyosha, who intends to become a monk. Ivan wishes to make clear to him what is involved in the acceptance of the religious view of the world.

"I've collected a great, great deal about Russian children, Alyosha. There was a little girl of five who was hated by her father and mother, 'most worthy and respectable people, of good education and breeding.' You see, I must repeat again, it is a peculiar characteristic of many people, this love of torturing children, and children only. To all other types of humanity these torturers behave mildly and benevolently, like cultivated and humane Europeans; but they are very fond of tormenting children, even fond of children themselves in that sense. It's just their defencelessness that tempts the tormentor, just the angelic confidence of the child who has no refuge and no appeal, that sets his vile blood on fire. In every man, of course, a demon lies hidden—the demon of rage, the demon of lustful heat at the screams of the tortured victim, the demon of lawlessness let off the chain, the demon of diseases that follow on vice—gout, kidney disease, and so on.

"This poor child of five was subjected to every possible torture by those cultivated parents. They beat her, thrashed her, kicked her for no reason till her body was one bruise. Then, they went to greater refinements of cruelty—shut her up all night in the cold and frost in a privy, and because she didn't ask to be taken up at night (as though a child of five sleeping its angelic, sound sleep could be trained to wake and ask), they smeared her face and filled her mouth with excrement, and it was her mother, her mother did this. And that mother could sleep, hearing the poor child's groans. Can you understand why a little creature, who can't even understand what's done to her, should beat her little aching heart with her tiny fist in the dark and the cold, and weep her meek, unresentful tears to dear, kind God to protect her? Do you understand that, friend and brother, you pious and humble novice? Do you understand why this infamy must be and is permitted? Without it, I am told, man could not have existed on earth, for he could not have known good and evil. Why should he know that diabolical good and evil when it costs so much? Why, the whole world of knowledge is not worth that child's prayer to 'dear, kind God'! I say nothing of the sufferings of grown-up people, they have eaten the apple, damn them, and the devil take them all! But these little ones!"

Dostoevsky then gives another instance of a serf-child of eight years thrown to dogs and torn to pieces before his mother's eyes to provide sport for a General, his owner, and so comes to his conclusion:

"Listen! I took the case of children only to make my case clearer. Of the other tears of humanity with which the earth is soaked from its crust to its centre, I will say nothing. I have narrowed my subject on purpose. I am a bug, and I recognise in all humility that I cannot understand why the world is arranged as it is. Men are themselves to blame, I suppose; they were given paradise, they wanted freedom, and stole fire from heaven, though they knew they would become unhappy, so there is no need to pity them. With my pitiful, earthly, Euclidean understanding, all I know is that there is suffering and that there are none guilty; that effect follows cause, simply and directly; that everything flows and finds its level—but that's only Euclidean nonsense. I know that, and I can't consent to live by it! What comfort is it to me that there are none guilty and that effect follows cause simply and directly, and that I know it—I must have justice, or I will destroy myself. And not justice in some remote infinite time and space, but here on earth, and that I could see myself. I have believed in it. I want to see it, and if I am dead by then, let me rise again, for if it all happens without me, it will be too unfair. Surely I haven't suffered, simply that I, my crimes and my sufferings, may manure the soil of the future harmony for somebody else. I want to see with my own eyes the hind lie down with the lion and the victim rise up and embrace his murderer. I want to be there when every one suddenly understands what it has all been for. All the religions of the world are built on this longing, and I am a believer. But then there are the children, and what am I to do about them? That's a question I can't answer. For the hundredth time I repeat, there are numbers of questions, but I've only taken the children, because in their case what I mean is so unanswerably clear. Listen! If all must suffer to pay for the eternal harmony, what have children to do with it, tell me, please? It's beyond all comprehension why they should suffer, and why they should pay for the harmony. Why should they, too, furnish material to enrich the soil for the harmony of the future? I understand solidarity in sin among men. I understand solidarity in retribution, too; but there can be no such solidarity with children. And if it is really true that they must share responsibility for all their father's crimes, such a truth is not of this world and is beyond my comprehension. Some jester will say, perhaps, that the child would have grown up and have sinned, but you see he didn't grow up, he was torn to pieces by the dogs, at eight years old. Oh, Alyosha, I am not blaspheming! I understand, of course, what an upheaval of the universe it will be, when everything in heaven and earth blends in one hymn of praise and everything that lives and has lived cries aloud: 'Thou art just, O Lord, for Thy ways are revealed.' When the mother embraces the fiend who threw her child to the dogs, and all three cry aloud with tears, 'Thou art just,

O Lord'! then, of course, the crown of knowledge will be reached and all will be made clear. But what pulls me up here is that I can't accept that harmony. And while I am on earth, I make haste to take my own measures. You see, Alyosha, perhaps it really may happen that if I live to that moment, or rise again to see it, I, too, perhaps, may cry aloud with the rest, looking at the mother embracing the child's torturer, 'Thou art just, O Lord!' but I don't want to cry aloud then. While there is still time, I hasten to protect myself and so I renounce the higher harmony altogether. It's not worth the tears of that one tortured child who beat itself on the breast with its little fist and prayed in its stinking outhouse, with its unexpiated tears to 'dear, kind God'! It's not worth it, because those tears are unatoned for. They must be atoned for, or there can be no harmony. But how? How are you going to atone for them? Is it possible? By their being avenged? But what do I care for avenging them? What do I care for a hell for oppressors? What good can hell do, since those children have already been tortured? And what becomes of the harmony, if there is hell? I want to forgive. I want to embrace. I don't want more suffering. And if the sufferings of children go to swell the sum of sufferings which was necessary to pay for the truth, then I protest that the truth is not worth such a price. I don't want the mother to embrace the oppressor who threw her son to the dogs! She dare not forgive him! Let her forgive him for herself, if she will, let her forgive the torturer for the immeasurable sufferings of her mother's heart. But the sufferings of her tortured child she has no right to forgive; she dare not forgive the torturer, even if the child were to forgive him! And if that is so, if they dare not forgive, what becomes of harmony? Is there in the whole world a being who would have the right to forgive and could forgive? I don't want harmony. From love for humanity I don't want it. I would rather be left with the unavenged suffering. I would rather remain with my unavenged suffering and unsatisfied indignation, *even if I were wrong*. Besides, too high a price is asked for harmony; it's beyond our means to pay so much to enter on it. And so I hasten to give back my entrance ticket, and if I am an honest man I am bound to give it back as soon as possible. And that I am doing. It's not God that I don't accept, Alyosha, only I must respectfully return Him the ticket."

This argument seems to me irrefutable. Who would consent to build a harmony that involved such suffering? Who could enjoy an eternity of bliss that had been purchased at such a price? Dostoevsky, in basing his case on the sufferings of children, has shown his complete understanding of the problem. And it is not the physical agony, but the abused confidence, the betrayed trust, that impresses one as the unforgivable and absolutely evil thing. All attempts to represent suffering as an imperfectly understood aspect of an eternal harmony break down before this argument. If life has a meaning, it is not to be found along those lines. Still less, of course, is it to be found in the idea, that seems to bring comfort to many people, that suffering is due to ignorance and maladjustment, and that the improved mankind of the future will be free from it. For this view really assumes, to begin with, that life is meaningless, and so the *problem* of suffering does not arise for it. It assumes, in fact, that life has come about by some sort of accident and will in due time come to an end. It has no transcendental significance. It is an episode between two eternities. Suffering is an unfortunate characteristic of life, so far as it has developed up till now. It has no meaning, any more than life itself has a meaning. But, since it is undesirable, we can hope that mankind will one day abolish it. In the meantime we can perhaps bear our sufferings and those of other people with more equanimity by reflecting on the healthy and happy generations of the future. As a solution of the problem discussed by Dostoevsky this is, of course, entirely puerile. But his problem does not exist for this view since it is, in a sense, already solved by the initial assumption that life has no transcendental significance. It is only when we regard life as more than an accident, and morality as more than an expression of the entirely arbitrary biological needs we happen to possess, that the problem of suffering arises at all.

Dostoevsky's argument leaves no room for any but the mystical solution of the problem of suffering and it is, in a sense, in rebellion against that. For the mystic claims to survey experience in the light of a higher consciousness than we normally possess, and he asserts that the problem of evil is unreal, that it arises from the limitations of the normal consciousness. The mystic claims, in effect, to have attained already the great moment of illumination of which Dostoevsky speaks. It is difficult for one who has never experienced the mystic vision to argue about it, but one can understand Dostoevsky's distrust of this way of abolishing the problem. If evil becomes unreal, what elements of our experience remain? Is not evil relative to our consciousness merely in the sense that everything else is?

THE PROBLEM OF SUFFERING

It is admitted that if our consciousness is radically changed our problems presumably cease to exist. But they equally cease to exist if we are annihilated. Does that fact illuminate anything? It is really very difficult to understand precisely what is claimed for the mystic vision. Nevertheless, it is not, I am convinced, to be lightly dismissed. In the writings of the great mystics there is a sincerity and profundity of spiritual experience that cannot be mistaken. And the fact that the experience they try to describe seems to be, in essentials, always the same experience, is certainly impressive. It is very remarkable that the mystic state of consciousness was experienced by Dostoevsky himself, and that he found it quite unforgettable and undeniable. It can, in his case, be described as a pathological condition for, when it occurred, it immediately preceded an epileptic fit. But to say this is to say very little, as Dostoevsky points out. It does not necessarily deprive an experience of all validity to find that it can only be experienced in exceptional bodily and mental conditions. And the mystic vision is by no means always accompanied by such conditions.

We may conclude, then, that, for the normal consciousness, the existence of what appears to be entirely gratuitous suffering is an insuperable objection to the belief that life has a meaning. The only escape from this conclusion depends on the acceptance of the validity and relevance of the mystic vision.

THE NECESSITY OF MYSTICISM

WE see that a belief in the validity of the mystic vision is a necessary presupposition if we wish to rationalize some of the most deep-seated elements of our general attitude towards life. But, perhaps, in using the phrase "mystic vision," I am being too definite. The mystic vision appears to be a quite definite clear-cut experience. It is incommunicable, but not vague. It is also, in its most indubitable form, very rare. But there is a state of mind which is perhaps not altogether unlike it, and which appears to be relatively common. I refer to the feeling, which perhaps occurs only rarely with certain men, that many of the things we normally accept as realities are somehow illusory. At such times we become aware, vaguely and transitorily, of our normal consciousness as being a limited thing. We are ready to admit the *possibility* that some of these limitations could conceivably be removed. Such a state can readily be induced by, for instance, pondering over the mystery of *time*. That the only existing thing is the ever-moving present, and that both the future and the past are non-existent, seems to be quite incredible. And yet the notion that time is unreal disturbs all the rest of our assumptions. There can be few men who have thought over this problem who do not feel that time is somehow incomprehensible. And yet there is nothing more fundamental in our consciousness than our awareness of time. Many, perhaps most, of the problems of metaphysics seem equally insoluble—they seem, in their essence, *ungraspable*. One becomes painfully aware of the fact that consciousness, in the form it has assumed in us, is limited. And this feeling makes the claims of the mystics less incredible. One becomes more ready to admit that the human consciousness may be capable of some radically new development and that, temporarily at any rate, some of the limitations that hem us in may be transcended.

Even if it does no more, this state of mind makes us regard certain arguments with a curious scepticism. We are often told, for example, that the immense spaces and times dealt with by modern astronomy make man "insignificant" in the universe. The earth, as a home for man is, in extent and duration, a mere speck in these immensities. Is it likely, we are asked, that man is part of a cosmic scheme when the cosmic scheme must be on so great a scale? It looks as if the whole history of man can be nothing but a negligible episode.

This argument certainly produces an effect, although the estimate of probability that is being appealed to is somewhat obscure. For in what way, precisely, is man's significance in the universe dependent on his physical dimensions and on the duration of his life? Yet that there is some connection is a very common impression. It was quite generally felt that a blow had been struck at man's dignity when Copernicus showed that the earth is not at the physical centre of the universe. The efforts that have been made since to show that the sun is, after all, at the centre of the Milky Way, springs from the same feeling. It is evident that man's significance is generally felt to be connected, in some way, with his physical size, duration, and position. Of these factors perhaps that of physical size is felt to be the least important, although Voltaire seems to have thought that men would be more admirable creatures if they were sixty feet high instead of six. The geometrical position of the earth is also a matter which has lost its old importance, especially now that the theory of a re-entrant space has been accepted. But the limited duration of man's life is still felt to be a serious obstacle to attributing cosmic importance to him. From the time of the Old Testament prophets the brevity of man's days has been regarded as an argument for his insignificance.

Yet the feeling persists that these arguments are all somehow irrelevant to the question of man's significance. This feeling is not due merely to the mind's stunned withdrawal from the contemplation of stellar distances and times—their millions of light-years and their millions of millions of years. It is due rather to an obscure awareness that the mind is, in some way, independent of space and time. This awareness has, of course, been made explicit in certain philosophies but, as a half-conscious assumption, it is very common. Most people, for instance, would find it very difficult to say what they mean by the past existence of the earth, before consciousness appeared. By the phrase "the universe, present, past and future," we mean what it is for consciousness, and any attempt to get outside consciousness seems to be an attempt to think thoughts that are not thinkable. Whether or not this feeling is justified is not now in dispute. It is, more or less consciously, shared by many people, and is one of the deep-seated but little recognised factors that condition a man's attitude towards the question of whether life has a meaning. This question is, indeed, associated with a complex of questions that very probably cannot be answered within the limitations of the normal consciousness. But the fact that these questions do not strike us as entirely meaningless is surely significant. If we accept the evolutionary theory of consciousness we must regard the mind as a sort of multiple plant, here in full flower, and there still in the bud. We have premonitions of developments that have not yet taken place. It is not unreasonable to assume that there are kinds of awareness which are still, as it were, in embryo within us. And the curiously elusive character of these questions, our feeling that they are at once important and ungraspable, suggests that their full understanding depends on a further growth of consciousness. People to whom this state of mind is familiar will not lightly dismiss the claims of the mystics. The assumption behind such claims will not be felt as *a priori* incredible.

HUMAN IMMORTALITY

It is possible that the problem of human immortality is a pseudo-problem. For if the mind is independent of time and space the notion of infinite duration obviously does not apply to it. For most of us, however, the notion that time is unreal is no more than a very occasional and vague intuition. To our normal consciousness the question of immortality remains a definite and important problem.

The question of man's cosmic significance is felt to be bound up with this question of immortality. Even if man be not immortal it is nevertheless possible, of course, that he forms an essential part of some eternal scheme. But our longing for a final harmony could not be met by such a scheme. To know that our life has a meaning, but that we shall never know the meaning, does not meet the kind of interest we take in the matter. It does, in truth, still leave our lives meaningless to us. If we regard all life as working towards some future harmony, then it is clear we must be present to witness the harmony. Otherwise we have been merely "manure," to use Dostoevsky's phrase. Thus, life cannot possess the sort of transcendent significance we are interested in unless we are immortal.

I would like to remark here how crude this way of envisaging the problem seems to be compared with the mystic solution. If we are to suppose some *future* harmony towards which all things are moving, at what date are we to suppose this harmony to be attained? Supposing we are immortal, how long do we exist before partaking of the harmony? And if it be said, as the Christian religion seems to say, that the harmony already exists (Heaven), and that death is our introduction to it, then when may we suppose it to have come into existence? It seems evident that the harmony must be supposed to be located either at the beginning or at the end of time, that is, outside time altogether. This would agree with the mystic assertion that life is justified now, and that the notion of time is irrelevant. The mystic vision, it would then appear, is a *timeless* vision. It is possible only when freed from the insistent space and time that limits the normal consciousness. This seems to be in accordance with the descriptions of their experience given by various mystics.

Assuming, however, that time is a reality, what are we to say about the question of human immortality? If we regard the mind as an aspect of the body, as being one form of its activities, then, of course, immortality is out of the question. We can only raise the question of immortality if we regard the mind as capable of existing independently of the body. This hypothesis is less easy to entertain than it was formerly. Our present physiological knowledge shows a much closer correlation between mental states and bodily changes than was before suspected. Both intelligence and character can, it appears, be fundamentally affected by suitable operations on the body. Even if these results lead us to believe that an indissoluble connection exists between mind and body, we are not thereby compelled, of course, to accept materialism. We are not forced to believe that the mind is *identical* with the body, or with any part of it. Indeed, the reduction of mind to matter remains as unintelligible as it ever was. But this fact is of no value for the hypothesis of immortality if we suppose that the nature of the mind-body connection, whatever it may be, is such that the mind cannot exist independently of the body. As there is nothing that forces us to make this assumption, we will not make it, but will consider what can be said for and against the hypothesis of human immortality on *a priori* grounds.

An argument against human immortality, which C. D. Broad, in his magnificent book on *The Mind and its Place in Nature*, rightly says has great influence on feeling, is the apparent random, wasteful, careless manner in which human beings come into the world. Besides the fact that so many human beings come into the world so casually, the result of a passing caprice or, perhaps, of a drunken frolic, we have to consider those that are born dead, are born idiotic, or horribly malformed. We have also to consider such indefensible abortions as Siamese twins and worse monsters. It would seem that, at best, Nature is utterly indifferent, and operates entirely without regard for human notions of beauty and dignity. It is difficult to believe that the slobbering and misshapen idiot, born of a drab in a ditch, is animated by an immortal soul.

The first part of this argument, that based on the casual way in which many human beings come into the world, need not have much weight with those who believe that life forms part of some great scheme. For we do not know what unimaginable combination of forces and events may have been necessary to produce what seems to us a casual incident. Also, we cannot argue the triviality of an effect from the apparent triviality of its cause. A forest fire may be started by a casual match. We could also suppose that the apparent cause is only part of the real cause. The physical coupling of two human beings, whether casual or deliberate, may be only part of what is required for the creation of a new mind. But the second part of the argument, that based upon the apparent unworthiness of so many human beings to survive, has wider ramifications. For if we deny immortality to some human beings, where are we to draw the line? If a certain level of intelligence and character is necessary for survival, how do we know what this level is? Might it not be that no human mind has yet appeared which reaches the required level? And if we adopt the other alternative and say that all human beings are immortal, where again are we to draw the line? It would appear that we must include not only the least developed races now existing, but also primitive man. Thus we would be led by insensible gradations to include the higher apes and, finally, shell-fish, microscopic organisms, and plants. The conclusion seems to be absurd.

Dr. Broad, who has given careful attention to this argument, thinks that there is very little in it. The argument, put simply, has three forms, (1) Oysters are not immortal; (2) We pass, by a series of insensible gradations, from oysters to men; (3) Therefore men are not immortal.

Now, in the first place, however gradual the transition from oysters to men may be, it must be admitted that there is a very great difference between these two ends of the chain. Men differ, in very important respects, from oysters. Now are those characteristics of oysters which make us deny them immortality characteristics which differentiate oysters markedly from men? If they are, then the argument from continuity proves nothing, for it is the differences that are important. Now when we reflect on our reasons for denying immortality to oysters we shall find, Dr. Broad thinks, that they are concerned with aspects where the oyster is markedly non-human. We may instance the feebleness of the oyster's mind, the poverty of his spiritual nature, the apparent triviality of his earthly destiny. It is because of these differences from his human successor that we are inclined to deny immortality to the oyster. The fact that there is continuity between the oyster and man, therefore, is quite compatible with the assertion that men are immortal and that oysters are not. If we accept this assertion, then the utmost the argument from continuity can do is to make us doubtful of the immortality of some intermediate types. We might hesitate, for example, about kangaroos.

The direction of the argument from continuity can, of course, be reversed. We can argue from the probable immortality of man to the less probable immortality of the oyster. The apparent absurdity of this argument seems to spring, not only from the characteristics of oysters, but also from their numbers. It is felt that the survival of every living creature is unlikely, if only on the ground that such vast numbers would be involved. But, as Dr. Broad says, we have no reason to suppose that the universe is conducted according to the Law of Parsimony. Indeed, we have very good evidence that it is not. The progress of astronomy was hindered by the fact that the Copernican theory, when its consequences were looked into, required the stars to be separated from one another by enormous distances. Astronomers of that day, unconsciously deriving their notions of the probabilities from farming considerations, could not believe that such a great waste of space was incurred. We now know that such notions of probability afford no clue to the structure of the universe. Nature shows no disposition to avoid large numbers.

There seems to be no conclusive argument against the immortality of man. Are there any good arguments for it? We may dismiss the arguments based on metaphysical principles and on ethical considerations, since it is generally agreed that they have failed. The immortality of man cannot be established on *a priori* grounds. We have to ask, therefore, whether there is any empirical evidence for it. This is a difficult question to answer, for we find, when we come to examine the evidence that has been put forth, that our estimate of it is influenced by notions of probability that may be altogether irrelevant. Many of the messages supposed to be received from discarnate spirits at spiritualistic séances, for instance, seem so crude, undignified, and downright silly, that they seem to bear evidence of their falseness on their face. Quite apart from other considerations, we reject them without further examination. But it may be that our notions about the spirit world are altogether too exalted. It may be that the shock of death reduces even the greatest human minds to a condition of relative imbecility, that an educated man forgets practically all he knows, and that a great poet becomes indistinguishable from the more insipid composers of Christmas card verses. The evidence adduced by spiritualists, if we take it seriously, certainly seems to point to this conclusion, and if we reject this evidence it must be on *a priori* grounds. We must be convinced that the universe is not as evil, or, at least, as imbecile, as the spiritualists would have us believe. But it is difficult to find any grounds that would justify this conviction. Why should we assume that the nature of the universe is consonant with our higher aspirations? We know, from our experience, that these aspirations are often defeated. There is sufficient evil in the world to make us doubt whether the general trend of things is towards good. Millions of men, for thousands of years, have found it perfectly consonant with their experience of the way the universe is governed to suppose that a hell forms part of its constitution, that an eternity of torment is part of the Divine economy. In comparison, the spiritualistic revelations are almost consoling. An eternity of happy imbecility is surely to be preferred to the intelligent appreciation of undying torments.

Dr. Broad, on the basis of his reading and of certain personal experiments in psychical research, is inclined to believe that there is a future life and that it is an imbecile form of existence. He supposes that there is a *psychic factor* which, in combination with a living organism, forms a mind. The psychic factor alone is not a mind, although it possesses mental characteristics. This psychic factor does, in some cases at any rate, survive bodily death. We can explain the really well-attested results of psychical research, Dr. Broad thinks, by supposing that disembodied psychic factors attach themselves temporarily to living brains—say the brains of mediums. A psychic factor thus becomes an element of a temporary mind. This temporary mind will have some of the characteristics of the medium and some of the characteristics of the mind of which it once formed part in life. This will explain the puzzling fact that so many communications from alleged discarnate minds, while revealing characteristics that belonged to those minds in life, also reveal characteristics which obviously belong to the medium.

The hypothesis of a psychic factor is put forward by Dr. Broad as the *minimum* hypothesis necessary to explain certain psychic phenomena. Alleged discarnate spirits are, he points out, singularly reticent about their present surroundings and activities. Such information as they give on these points is so extraordinarily silly that it obviously comes from the medium. It would seem that whatever survives death is something incapable of further experience. Its memory, on the other hand, seems to be unimpaired. Thus it has mental characteristics, but it is not what we call a mind. Dr. Broad thinks that the established facts of psychic research warrant this hypothesis, but that they do not compel us to go beyond it.

In order to accept Dr. Broad's theory it is obviously necessary to overcome our desire to believe in a future life which is better than our present life. No one can derive consolation from the idea that he will persist as a psychic factor, for the most part completely inanimate, but perhaps, for brief intervals, able to manifest certain memories when attached to the brain of some medium. There is little to choose between this kind of survival and complete annihilation. From the point of view of our hopes and aspirations we should have to decide that the universe is a very disappointing affair. And if we do this, why should we not go further and accept the whole spiritualistic revelation of a spirit world where they smoke cigars, take dogs for walks, and play practical jokes? Why attribute all such information to the silliness of the medium? What ideal of beauty, of dignity, are we still clinging to, and what is our justification for clinging to any such ideal? How can we say what statement is probable, or not probable, about such a universe? It is, of course, perfectly reasonable to say that there is a future life, but that our desires afford no clue to its nature. Then every conceivable hypothesis as to its nature becomes equally probable. It must be admitted that our experience of life, surveyed reasonably, lends equal support to any hypothesis.

Yet we do not, in fact, regard all hypotheses as equally credible. The hypothesis that the universe is ruled by a wholly beneficent creator presents grave difficulties, but it is less incredible than the hypothesis that it is ruled by a malignant devil. Yet we do not arrive at this conclusion from some sort of statistical survey of experience. It would be impossible to maintain that the happiness of the world outweighs its suffering. Our feeling that good is more fundamental in the universe than is evil is not the product of experience. It is a conviction that is arrived at intuitively. And this conviction can persist through much suffering, even when the suffering appears to be quite gratuitous and meaningless. This fact is surely significant.

Much of the greatest art in the world, that which most moves us, owes its ascendancy over us to this conviction. In such works suffering is present, sometimes profound suffering, but it has been transmuted. It has, in some sense, been justified. Out of evil has come good. And it is to be observed that the effect of such works is not to be described as merely consolatory. It would be much more true to say that they bestow *understanding*. We agree, for the time being, that suffering has here received a final resolution. It has been related to something more fundamental than itself.

This quality in great art is probably not unconnected with the mystic vision. It is probable that the peculiar state of awareness that is communicated by some great art is of the same kind as the mystic revelation. Under the influence of such art we dwell, temporarily, in a region where all our questions are answered or, rather, where they no longer exist. Such art seems to be, in itself, a justification of life. I believe that this is not an illusion. I believe that such art does spring from a level of understanding or awareness akin to that of the mystic. Perhaps the clearest examples of art of this magnitude are to be found in music and, in particular, in the later music of Beethoven. This music, as we see from the sort of references that are made to it, probably does convey, to many people, a state of awareness that we can only call mystical. In discussing this question, therefore, we may confine ourselves to the example presented by this music, since the issues involved are perhaps more clearly presented here than anywhere else.

A DISSERTATION ON BEETHOVEN

It is probable that our age is able to criticize Beethoven more adequately than has been possible at any time during the last hundred years. The criticism of his contemporaries is relatively valueless. Some of them could appreciate certain outward characteristics of Beethoven's music, but the development in Beethoven of a radically new conception of the whole art of music is something that even the most sensitive of them could not be expected fully to perceive. Their approach to music rested upon certain assumptions—assumptions so deep rooted that they were, for the most part, unconscious; a music which rested on different assumptions was, in reality, inaudible. That Beethoven was greatly honoured and applauded in his own lifetime is quite true, but the essential characteristic of his music, that which differentiates it from all other music, was only dimly perceived. He was considered, at most, as a superior Mozart or Haydn. Such misunderstandings were inevitable. In the early nineteenth century Bach was practically unknown. Music as conceived by Mozart and Haydn was what was meant by music. Beethoven's greatest admirers realized in him a superior creative force, but not that this force was employed to entirely different ends. It is doubtful whether the realization of this difference is even now at all general. Musical criticism is still chiefly a matter of generalities and unilluminating metaphors. The *objects* of musical criticism have not yet been properly discriminated, and nowhere is this technical deficiency more apparent than in the voluminous literature dealing with Beethoven.

In the age immediately following that of Beethoven, the Victorian Age, criticism was swamped by morality. A great artist had to be remarkable for the elevation of his style and the nobility of his sentiments, these terms being given the meanings they bear for vigorous, prosperous, commercial people. It was during this period that the legend was formulated of Beethoven as the lofty moralist and the nobly renunciatory lover. Except for the absence of whiskers he was turned into a Victorian celebrity of the most approved type. This legend still persists; and it is still a shock to many readers of Mr. Thayer's immense *Life of Beethoven* when they reach the patiently worked out conclusion of that great work that Beethoven was not an English gentleman. The Victorians had no serious curiosity about Beethoven the man, and they seem to have had little more about his music. In both cases they were chiefly concerned to indulge emotions of which they approved. But it is true that a critical appreciation of Beethoven's music was difficult; the qualities that made it obscure to his contemporaries made it obscure also to the Victorians. From the musicians, such as Schumann and Wagner, came little but vague dithyrambic phrases, conveying nothing except the fact that they greatly admired this music. From the cultured critic, such as Sir George Grove, there was much admirable criticism of details, but no apparent understanding of what was for Beethoven, the whole *raison d'être* of his work.

We are at present in a better position to appreciate

both Beethoven the man and Beethoven the musician. In the first task we are greatly helped by our relative moral freedom. The Victorian ideals appear to us now as unduly restricted and remote from reality. Their function in keeping together an individualistic commercial community is now too apparent. The Victorian standards of excellence are no more applicable to a profound and elemental genius such as Beethoven than their Biblical cosmogony is applicable to the real universe. It is for that reason that Mr. Thayer's proof that Beethoven was not a gentleman has now lost much of its horror. The task of appreciating Beethoven's music has been made easier for us by the popularity of Wagner. For Wagner, like Beethoven, used music as a medium for expressing aspects of himself, and as a record of his spiritual development. Neither Wagner nor Beethoven tried to compose works of art in the Mozartian sense. They were not concerned to make beautiful music, but to express something beautifully through music. This conception of a musical composition as a method of conveying a certain apprehension of life was not thoroughly grasped by Beethoven's contemporaries. It has been grasped by us chiefly because of its exemplification in the work of Wagner. What Wagner had to express was readily understood. He was much nearer to our common humanity than was Beethoven. His emotions and spiritual experiences were those of the ordinary sensual man. From the delirium of sexual love to that craving for the refreshing ministrations of white-robed angels that follows exhaustion by fever, he expressed the whole spiritual progress from youthful pride of life to rapt and holy contemplation as it is understood by the sensualist. Such experiences are

A DISSERTATION ON BEETHOVEN

within the reach of all. Once Wagner's unusual way of writing music was understood there were no further difficulties. He showed, in a way that everybody could understand, that music could be an extraordinarily powerful and direct means of expressing a personal vision of life. His conception of music was really the same as Beethoven's; his musical language was different, and what he had to say was different; but he, like Beethoven, used music as a means of personal expression. By doing this so obviously he has made clear the main lines upon which an investigation of Beethoven's music should proceed. Beethoven's music is to be studied as the record of a spiritual development: as, in fact, one gigantic piece of "Programme" music, to give this term of somewhat extended meaning.

The difference between "programme" music and "pure" music may be variously defined, but for our present purpose it is useful to find the distinction in the law governing the movement or development of a composition. We may say that the programme composer is concerned with a psychological as well as a musical development in his composition. That there is such a thing as a purely musical development must be admitted. Any musical phrase is susceptible of a large number of developments, but not of *any* development. The choice depends upon the musical instinct of the composer. He will, normally, regard many developments as admissible, although sometimes, as in some completely successful melodies, it seems as if the latter part were uniquely conditioned by the first part. The laws of development which make a musical composition a unity instead of a haphazard succession of notes are, of course, psychological. They cannot be anything else; but we know, at present, nothing about these laws. It is not these laws to which we refer when we speak of the psychological development of the composition. In a composition which obeys a psychological development of the kind that makes it programme music a further principle of selection has been brought into play besides that exercised by the purely musical instinct. As a rough analogy we may liken the process to that of a poet who selects amongst the words having the necessary rhythm and rhyme those that have the appropriate meaning. The programme composer has to choose amongst the developments that are musically admissible—whether the developments be the answers of a fugue or the second subjects of a sonata or some less easily classifiable development—those that shall also carry on and elucidate the psychological meaning of the composition. The composition must be not only beautiful but meaningful. An examination of the phrases tried and rejected in Beethoven's late notebooks shows how extremely arduous such a two-fold search may be.

The value of such music is therefore two-fold. It exists not only to create an "aesthetic emotion" but also to communicate a spiritual experience. Its value, therefore, is largely dependent on the value of the spiritual experience that inspires it. For music of this kind to be great its composer must be, in the fullest sense of the term, a great man. He must be capable of experiences such as only the highest order of human being can attain to. For many people Beethoven is, in this sense, the greatest artist who ever lived. They do not say that his music is more beautiful than that of all other composers, but they do say that its spiritual content is more profound and more valuable.

A DISSERTATION ON BEETHOVEN

The great difficulty in criticising Beethoven's music is to do justice to its spiritual content. It is here that shallowness in the critic will infallibly reveal itself. The fact that the critic must use words is, in any case, a hindrance. For language, owing to the fact that it was developed primarily as an instrument for use in practical affairs, is extremely poor in names for subjective states; and an experience which can be conveyed quite definitely and convincingly in music can be described only vaguely or metaphorically in words. It is partly for this reason that literary descriptions of music are amongst the most intolerable things in life. Turgenev's remark that music begins where words leave off, or Mendelssohn's remark that music is a much more definite language than the language of words, are both perfectly sound. The first difficulty that confronts the musical critic is, therefore, well-nigh insuperable. It is not, perhaps, so much true that writers of descriptive programmes for concerts are more imbecile than other men, but that they are attempting the almost impossible. In the case of Beethoven the difficulty is greatly increased by the fact that the experiences he wished to convey, particularly in his last period, belong to the greatest heights and depths that the spirit of man has yet reached. This man passed through one of the profoundest spiritual developments of which we have any record. His "revelation" which he said was higher than all wisdom and philosophy, would, if expressed in words, indubitably be classed as mystical, and probably be found unintelligible. He had the immense advantage of having music as his medium of expression. Even so, there are indications that he was reaching the limits of what music could carry—music, that is, that was to be bodied forth in physical sounds.

The history of Beethoven's spiritual development is, in essentials, similar to the history of their development which is given by the great mystics. A period of struggle and defiance is followed by a period where all hope is lost, the period that has been called the black night of the soul. This period, which may last for years, is succeeded, in some inexplicable way, by the final period of illumination where all conflicts are resolved, although none of the elements of experience are denied or forgotten. Beethoven's music, it seems to me, unmistakably reflects these three stages. From the Eroica Symphony till the years of silence that fell upon him in 1810, Beethoven's music is essentially the record of a conflict, the assertion of his creative power and will against some sort of hypostatised fate. "I will take Fate by the throat," he wrote, when the threat of his impending deafness made him first aware of the necessity of heroic assertion. Again and again, in the compositions of this period, we find this attitude expressed. Beethoven had found within himself a mighty endurance and an unconquerable will, and in doing so he thought he had found the key to life. Suffering is to be countered by courage—that was Beethoven's simple and heroic formula. But this, obviously, is a way of life only for the elect. For the great bulk of mankind such a solution, even if it be, in truth, a solution, is impossible of attainment. And Beethoven himself found that it was not sufficient. There came a period when he found that his defiance and self-assertion were unavailing. For nearly a decade he was silent; none of his great works were originated and matured during this period. But

A DISSERTATION ON BEETHOVEN

we have one composition, the Hammerclavier Sonata, which stands as a sort of memorial to this stage of his development. It is a truly amazing expression of courage without hope. The victorious quality, which had characterised so much of Beethoven's music, is here entirely absent. Nowhere in Beethoven's music is sorrow so despairing as in the slow movement of this sonata, and the last movement, one of the most violent and emphatic of all Beethoven's movements, expresses nothing but a blind, indomitable insistence on sheer existence, when no purpose and no meaning is left in life. This sonata stands at the end of a spiritual process. Nothing, we feel, can come from it.

But at the time Beethoven wrote this sonata he had already passed beyond it. He had begun to enter upon his greatest creative period, the third and final stage of his spiritual development. In the music of this period we have a music quite unlike any other music. It reveals to us what we can only describe as new states of awareness, a new degree of consciousness. What Beethoven has here done is to make a synthesis of all his experience. The different elements of life are no longer presented as contrasting, but as strangely unified. Yet nothing is abandoned or fogotten, and the pulse that beats in the last quartets, for example, is as vigorous as anywhere in Beethoven's music. This is the music that so many writers have called "mystical" or "metaphysical," and it is certain that the effect of this music, its power of transporting us to a region where all our discords are not ignored, but resolved, seems to have much in common with the mystic vision. Probably there is nothing else in art which comes so near to expressing what the mystics themselves confess is inexpressible.

The importance of this art, from our present point of view, is that it makes credible the possibility of the complete mystic vision. Under the influence of this music it seems to be possible to imagine a state of consciousness for which the problem of suffering is resolved. And the effect is permanent. We have caught but a glimpse of this new state of awareness; we have but dimly apprehended this new and complete synthesis of all experience, but the revelation, partial as it may be, is quite unforgettable.

Whether or not the art that possesses this quality is the greatest art is an ambiguous question. Also, it is not a question of great importance. What is important is that such art does exist, and that it convinces us of its complete authenticity. We are convinced, indeed, that the states of consciousness here depicted are in the main line of man's spiritual development. They are not freakish. The effect of such art, therefore, is immensely to reinforce the case for mysticism, if we agree that such art springs from a state of awareness akin to the mystic vision. It would then appear that the chief reason for the "incommunicability" of the mystic vision is the fact that the mystic vision, like many other great human experiences, can only be fully communicated by a great artist. It belongs to that region of experience with which propositional language is unable to deal. This is the region of art, and is the reason why art is not superfluous. In the person of the late Beethoven we had, I believe, an artist who was also a mystic, and the combination has given us the most profound and valuable of all the revelations of art. In forming any conclusion as to the meaning of life we must allow these revelations to play their part.

THE SCIENTIFIC OUTLOOK

AT a time, not so very long ago, when scientific men confined themselves to science and refrained from publicly expressing their ideas on things in general, it was customary to talk about science and art as if they were activities entirely different from one another. Indeed, the scientific mind and the artistic mind were often presented to us as being at opposite poles. We now know that this clear-cut division does not exist. There is still, it is true, the kind of scientific specialist who seems to be wholly absorbed in amassing facts. This type flourishes, however, chiefly on the less developed sciences, where the crying need is precisely for more facts. In the more developed sciences, and particularly in mathematical physics, we see more and more clearly that aesthetic considerations play a very important part. Science, in its most developed form has, indeed, many of the characteristics of an art. And the men who are concerned with these sciences make no secret of the fact that their motives and satisfactions are very much those of the artist. It sometimes happens, indeed, that the choice between two theories, covering the same region of phenomena, seems to be dictated by aesthetic considerations. We would expect, therefore, that, in these regions, the work of a great scientific creator would exhibit personal qualities akin to those exhibited by a great work of art.

But the sense in which the work of a man of science

may be described as personal is not at all easy to make out. The personal character of a work of art is easily recognized, and it would seem that the essential difference between science and art lies precisely in the fact that science is impersonal, whereas art is not. Yet no man of science can feel quite happy with this classification. He perceives, or thinks he can, individuality in the contributions to the same branch of science made by various scientific men. Are we to suppose that these differences are superficial, a matter of mannerisms or the recurrence of favourite devices, or may it be that the great scientific creator expresses a vision which is as unique and personal as that of the great artist? It seems very difficult to admit the latter possibility. The laws of nature are presumably independent of the mind, and in discovering a law of nature the man of science is revealing the constitution of the universe but not the constitution of his mind. A law of nature is not an expression of its discoverer's personality, and this remains true even if we accept the modern surmise that all that we have been accustomed to call laws of nature have been contributed by the mind. For this can be true only in the sense that space and time, on some metaphysical theories, are contributed by the mind, and the mind here referred to is something much more basic and general than any mind to which we attribute individuality. The problem is not illuminated even when we remember that for every law of nature a more complicated one could be substituted that would work quite as well. It is true that the human criterion of simplicity is responsible for the actual forms in which laws of nature are enunciated, but since this criterion is presumably the same for all human beings, we have no room here for individuality. Scientific theories, on the other hand, as distinguished from laws, have seemed to many writers to be much more arbitrary creations. That the planets move round the sun in ellipses would seem to be the impersonal expression of a fact. That this motion should be attributed to a force of gravitation would seem to be the outcome of Sir Isaac Newton's early training and the native characteristics of his mind. The proof would appear to be in the fact that a different mind with a different training, that of Albert Einstein, accounts for this motion in an entirely different way. The interesting but unanswerable question arises whether Einstein, in Newton's place, would have invented an alternative theory of gravitation. In short, is the present position of science, like the present position of the arts, due to a series of historical accidents?

The history of science does not enable us to answer this question. There have been too few really great geniuses, and they have been too far removed in time from one another. There have been instances, of course, of independent thinkers hitting on the same theory simultaneously. And there have been instances of quite different theories covering the same facts successfully for years. It might be thought that the only difference here is that, in the one case, scientific knowledge is in a state that makes the next step in advance unambiguous, whereas in the second case there are not sufficient relevant facts to hand, and alternatives are therefore possible. Nevertheless, the feeling remains that some men of science are irreplaceable. Einstein has said, of some of Gauss's work, that if he had not thought of it, it would never have been thought of. Yet there are scientific theories, and of the highest quality, of which we feel that, whether their historical author had existed or not, they were certain to be invented. We feel about Newton's law of gravitation that it was bound to come. Of such theories it is hard to believe that they owe anything to the personality of their authors, in the sense that a Beethoven quartet is certainly something much more than the inevitable outcome of a musical "movement." And Einstein's theory is so far from being an expression of the *Zeit-geist* that it is still a difficult matter to provide it with an ancestry. The difficulty of understanding in what sense a scientific theory may be regarded as an individual achievement may be due to the inadequacy of science as a medium of personal expression. A system of logic, if it be perfect, can reveal nothing individual; it is only by his mistakes that one logician can be differentiated from another. So far as a work of science exhibits "reasoning power" it may show ability but not personality. But a scientific theory also reveals something of its author's imagination, and this is a quality susceptible of marked individual differences. It still reveals much less, of course, than does a work of art, but this makes the difference one of degree rather than one of kind. It follows, therefore, that a scientific theory may be a unique and personal thing. The quality of the imagination shown may be commonplace or it may be original. In the first case the author of the theory does not strike us as irreplaceable, although, if he had not existed, his work might have consumed the labours of several generations. In the second case we feel that, as a result of that man's work, science is moving in a direction it might never have taken. Whether the "objectivity" of science and the possibility of a final explanation of the universe may still be preserved by saying that all paths lead to the same goal may be left to the philosophers to discuss.

The view that a scientific theory may be a unique and personal thing suggests that criticism might endeavour to deduce, from the characteristics of a work of science, those qualities in the author that were concerned in its creation. The analysis of works of science from this point of view has never been seriously undertaken. Scientific men are popularly regarded as being very much alike. They are all supposed to possess the "scientific mind," an entity which has never been exhaustively described, but whose most marked characteristics, in popular expositions, seem to be its appetite for facts and its love of logical reasoning. A very slight acquaintance with men of science is sufficient to show that this account is misleading, and to cast grave doubt on the existence of anything that can be called a scientific mind. Perhaps Henry Cavendish comes nearest to the popular idea of what a scientific man should be. He went as far as the patient collection of facts and acute deductions from them could carry a man. But there seems to be nothing in common between him and Kepler, a man with an imagination that would not have disgraced the more hysterical species of poet, and who would probably be regarded by a modern astronomer as totally unfitted for scientific research. Nevertheless, the actual scientific achievements both of Cavendish and Kepler might have been produced by very different men. We become more aware of this elusive personal quality when we consider the work of such a man as James Clerk Maxwell, and it seems likely that the study of his life, like that of many artists, helps in the intimate understanding of his work. He is a favourable case for such a study, for his work was of the first importance, was extremely original, and was the product of a remarkably homogeneous nature.

A DISSERTATION ON MAXWELL

It is not usual to look for the rarer spirits of mankind amongst men of science. Scientific men are treated very much as being what Nietzsche said they were—namely, instruments. It is cheerfully conceded that they are abstruse reasoners and curiously able to understand complicated mechanisms, but as leaders of humanity, as men with any real understanding of the mystery of life, with any real knowledge of all that most troubles and concerns the spirit, they are regarded as negligible. One expects the biography of a great mathematician to be interesting in very much the same way as the biography of a performing dog. Besides his marvellous aptitude for complicated tricks, he seems to have had all the usual affections. And supposing that the mathematician were more, supposing that he had what Einstein calls a truly religious feeling in face of nature, as the great artist has in face of his art, it is hardly to be expected that this, his inmost and secret inspiration, could be expressed in his work. Yet it can be expressed —by the quality of his imagination. With Maxwell, in particular, we are forced to conclude that his work, rigorously scientific as it is, impresses his readers as having something of the indefinable spiritual significance of a great work of art. The references to Maxwell in the writings of scientific men are, from this point of view, exceedingly interesting. His work has affected their imaginations in a way to which it is hard to find a parallel. He is easily, to physicists, the most magical figure of the nineteenth century, yet it would be impossible to say that, in what is generally known as scientific ability, he was superior to all other men of his time. But indeed we have only to study these references to find that it is the quality of his imagination that awakens this curious respect, and something very like affection, in the minds of those who never met him. A recently published autobiography by Professor Pupin shows this remarkable phenomenon very clearly. We see an imaginative youth, attracted powerfully but inexplicably by the curious quality he sensed in Maxwell's electro-magnetic theory of light, starting off on a veritable "quest of the ideal" in his attempt to master that theory. With the naïvety of a lover or a religious devotee, he goes to the places where Maxwell had been, confusedly hoping that something in the atmosphere and surroundings would help him to seize the essential quality of the great man's mind. And he explained the theory to his mother in such wise that that old lady was moved to comment: "He must be one of God's saints." Professor Pupin is but one of many disciples of Maxwell who experienced the same fervour and glow, the same reverence for the man. Even Einstein, who is at least fully comparable with Maxwell as a scientific genius, has this same reverent affection for him. In his trinity of great men, Newton, Faraday, Maxwell, there is reason to suspect that Maxwell comes first. That this feeling towards Maxwell on the part of so many men of science comes wholly from his work, in complete ignorance of his life, we should be reluctant to assert; that it comes partly from his work we are convinced. To understand the effect of Maxwell's work we should probably have to share the ideas of the people to whom it was new. But a parallel, in our own time, is furnished by the relativity theory. The general effect is one of imaginative enfranchisement accompanied by a greater degree than ever before of comprehension. We have reached a deeper level of understanding of the universe, and at the same time the universe has become more mysterious. Both the light and the darkness are essential to the pleasure we take in a scientific theory. When science is complete it will also be uninteresting. The point has been well expressed by Maxwell himself when he says that "It is a universal condition of the enjoyable that the mind must believe in the existence of a law and yet have a mystery to move about in."

Maxwell's theory appeared at a time when the Newtonian ideas still dominated physical science. The enthusiasm that greeted the appearance of Newton's work did not quite correspond to the joy that Maxwell defines. The contemporary attitude was well expressed in the lines:

> Nature and Nature's laws lay hid in night:
> God said, Let Newton be; and all was light.

It was felt that mystery was banished from the universe. Its laws had been discovered; all that remained was to work them out in detail. And for generations the task of working them out went on. The ideal of science was to explain everything in terms of the Newtonian mechanics. As a by-product of this endeavour may be mentioned the rehabilitation of materialism as a philosophy. To know the fundamental laws of the universe would certainly, we may suppose, make for happiness, and a scientific man might consider his life well spent in applying these laws to one particular case after another. But if Maxwell's definition of the enjoyable be accepted, something would have been felt to be lacking. This something, to many minds, was provided by his electro-magnetic theory of light. The explanation came, as it were, from a totally unsuspected region. A new direction and fresh vistas were opened up. A new way of thinking about the universe became imperative, a way so new that Lord Kelvin, to the end of his long life, was not able to adopt it. And neither Maxwell nor his immediate followers fully realized what had happened. Maxwell himself made efforts to reconcile the new outlook with the old by endeavouring to give mechanical interpretations to his equations. That he should do so was quite characteristic of Maxwell. He combined, to an extraordinary degree, a sceptical critical faculty with a most tenacious conservatism. But in the present case more than mere conservatism was involved. The Newtonian mechanics were for Maxwell, as for most other English physicists of his time, the basis of comprehension of natural phenomena. These English men of science had an incurable yearning to "picture" the way things worked, and their pictures, of course, had to be made up out of entities with which they were familiar. They could not rest in the position of the Continental physicists, who were quite content not to penetrate behind the equations. From our present point of view this was a kind of stupidity in Maxwell, an uncritical acceptance of certain criteria of explanation. It is possible now to feel surprised that Maxwell did not more fully realize what he had done, that an imagination so bold should not have been bolder. But Maxwell is a clear instance of the fact that

A DISSERTATION ON MAXWELL

even a very great genius is conditioned by his age. It is for this reason that Maxwell's life is so fascinating. There can be few instances where the individual quality of a man and the influence of his age are so readily separable.

That Maxwell was some kind of mystic is apparent from many of his remarks and letters. In this, as in other ways, he was akin to Faraday. This mystic awareness was not the result of some catastrophic experience. "I have been thinking," he says, "how very gently I have been always dealt with. I have never had a violent shove in all my life." But, however gradually, he passed from a state where the world had no meaning to a state where it was full of purpose. In his own words: "Long ago I felt like a peasant in a country overrun with soldiers, and saw nothing but carnage and danger. Since then I have learned at least that some soldiers in the field die nobly, and that all are summoned there for a cause." This consciousness of a purpose, of something greater than himself manifesting itself through him and all men, remained with Maxwell to the end of his life. We may explain it in various ways. It is possible that a man like Maxwell, in his normal moments, is as much bewildered as other people by those rare occasions when his genius, without let or hindrance, manifests itself freely. In these exalted states Maxwell felt that the self he knew was not alone involved. He says, "What is done by what is called myself is, I feel, done by something greater than myself in me." And yet there was a serenity about Maxwell which suggests that his work was the result of a slow and powerful development rather than of sudden flashes of "genius." The only clue that Maxwell offers is probably incomprehensible except to those who have had something of the same experience. He offers it as his "nostrum." "An abandonment of wilfulness without extinction of will, but rather by means of a great development of will, whereby, instead of being consciously free and really in subjection to unknown laws, it becomes consciously acting by law and really free from the interference of unrecognized laws."

In these statements by Maxwell we have records of his own direct experience. It was natural to so loyal and conservative a man, brought up in the nineteenth century in an orthodox Christian household, that he should try to give these experiences an orthodox religious interpretation. Yet, with all the gentleness and sympathy of Maxwell's references to the current religious doctrines, we are left with a vague doubt whether he was ever what could be called a believer. He seems to have believed both more and less than the Church required. But, with his strong veneration for tradition, he found it difficult to be entirely ruthless in his criticisms of these matters. Again like Faraday, he had no sufficient confidence in human reason to attribute more than a limited validity to its conclusions. It is the first duty of a thinker, said John Stuart Mill, to follow his intellect to whatever conclusions it may lead. Maxwell would not do that. He would not tolerate loose thinking on matters that he thought about, but, as every mystic must, he would distrust the conclusions of reason rather than his intuitive certainties. Even his scientific work was the outcome much more of intuition than of reason. As a mathematician Maxwell was by no means infallible; on the other hand, his intuitive grasp of a physical problem has never been excelled. His strong instinct would carry him through to the correct result, although, when he came to prove the result, his reasoning might be faulty. It is impossible to define what is meant by "the intuitive grasp of a physical problem." Relevant factors are seized and associated in relevant ways, but the relevance is with respect to an end not yet reached. Perhaps we may liken the process to Beethoven's constant tinkering with a theme until at last his instinct assured him that it was pregnant with the developments he had not yet composed. With Maxwell the elements on which he lays stress are not always the obviously important ones. Platitudes, in his hands, could take on a deep meaning. He had the critical faculty in its highest sense, the delicate discrimination of the significant. It was this faculty that enabled him to supply unexpectedly easy proofs of complicated problems.

His scientific work, however, afforded only a partial manifestation of this faculty. His comments on philosophic ideas and on works of literature show the same discrimination. And it is characteristic of Maxwell that nearly everything he reads suggests some general reflection. As a light specimen we may quote from his criticism of "Festus," by Philip James Bailey, a forgotten poem which nevertheless was widely read in 1849, when Maxwell was nineteen. After a destructive analysis of the poem Maxwell tries to account for its popularity.

"People read the book and wonder, why?
"It is not read for the sake of the story—that is plain; nor for the clearness with which certain principles are developed, nor for the consistency of the

book, nor for the variety of the characters; there must, therefore, be something overpoweringly attractive to hold you to the book. Some say he has fine thoughts, sufficient to set up fifty poets; to which some may answer, Where are they? Read it in a spirit of cold criticism, and they vanish. There is not one that is not either erroneous, absurd, German, common or *daft*. Where lies the beauty? In the reader's mind. The author has evidently been thinking when he wrote it, and that not in words, but inwardly. The *benevolent reader* is compelled to think too, and it is so great a relief to the reader to get out of wordiness that he can put up with insanity, absurdity, profanity, and even inanity, if by so doing he can get into *rapport* with one who is so transcendental, and yet so easy to follow, as the poet. When Galileo set his lamp a-swinging by breathing on it, his power lay in the relation between the interval of his breaths and the time of vibration; so in Festus the mind that begins to perceive that his train of thoughts is that of the poem is readily made to follow on."

His critical faculty was never in abeyance. Even as a schoolboy he was keenly aware of the idiosyncrasies of his school-fellows and masters. He gives one always the impression of being very self-contained, watchful and alert. In spite of his conservatism no man was less at the mercy of words. He was curiously aware, ironically aware, of his own loyalty. Thus we find amongst his notes for future reading: "Kant's Critique of Pure Reason, read with a determination to make it agree with Sir William Hamilton," Hamilton being one of his teachers for whom he had great respect. If Maxwell must be classed as a mystic, as it is very probable, his mysticism certainly did not take the form of omphaloskepsis. "Objectivity alone," he says, "is favourable to the free circulation of the soul. But let the Object be real and not an Image of the mind's own creating, for Idolatry is Subjectivity with respect to gods."

Maxwell had all the equipment of the ordinary man of science, and something more. He differed from other men by being more inclusive, by being aware of more things. Maxwell's mysticism is primarily a greater degree of awareness. He had the perceptions of the artist as well as those of the man of science; very little that the soul can experience was strange to him. His scientific originality gives one the impression of springing from a richer context of ideas and perceptions than other men possess. Everything that he did came from the same centre. "Harmonious" is the word his friends used in trying to describe him. It is impossible to describe Maxwell as a scientific specialist with artistic tastes. That would be to miss the essential quality of the man. It would be more just to say that Maxwell gives the impression, not of having special gifts, but of possessing a heightened consciousness. Throughout we feel in contact with a mind more perceptive and more penetrating than our own, a mind in a higher state of awareness than our own. And possibly that is why his electro-magnetic theory of light seemed to his followers not only an interesting scientific advance but, in the quality of its originality, something of a superhuman revelation.

NEW PRINCIPLES

MAXWELL is the first man whose work takes us outside the Newtonian scheme. This fact was not fully realised by himself nor, perhaps, by any of his contemporaries, for the hope persisted for some years that a mechanical explanation would be given of Maxwell's Electromagnetic Theory of Light. It was only after repeated attempts had failed that electricity was finally accepted as a fundamental entity, as something that could not be reduced to mechanical terms. This discovery ushered in the modern period. It was realised, for the first time, that the concepts given by Newton were insufficient to cover the whole of physical phenomena. Since then the breakaway from the Newtonian system has become almost complete. None of the Newtonian concepts are now regarded as fundamental. The bricks out of which Newton tried to build the material universe have been replaced by others. But Newton's outlook on science has become more and more the outlook of scientific men. His insight into the nature of science, the perfect purity of his scientific mind, have never been equalled.

In order to understand the modern scientific outlook we must know something of the Newtonian scheme it has replaced. It is interesting, also, in connection with our general enquiry into the nature of the scientific mind, its motives and satisfactions, to enquire into Newton's attitude towards science. Was he primarily seeking for truth? What did he mean by truth? Was he an artist? Could he have said, as Einstein has said of himself, that his scientific speculations sprang from a profound religious impulse? The fact is that none of these descriptions fit Newton. His attitude towards science is more elusive, and yet somehow more satisfactory, than any of these. He had not only the greatest, but also the most interesting, mind in the history of science.

Not only have the Newtonian conceptions of time, space, mass, force, etc., been replaced by the concepts of relativity theory, but even the fundamental principle of continuity, in which he believed, has now been almost completely abandoned. Quantum Theory, which covers all the fundamental atomic phenomena, supposes that Nature passes from one state to another, not in a continuous manner, but by little finite jumps. Moreover, these jumps cannot be predicted. When an electron in an atom jumps from one orbit to another, for example, we cannot say which orbit it will jump to. The most we can do is to give the chances on each of its possible jumps. We can specify the probability that the electron will make one jump rather than another. We cannot say what it is *bound* to do.

This fact has led to the formulation of a very important principle—Heisenberg's Principle of Indeterminacy, or, as it is sometimes called, the Uncertainty Principle. This principle asserts that a particle may have position, or it may have velocity, but it cannot in any exact sense have both. The precise status of this principle is still somewhat obscure. The younger workers in physics are, on the whole, convinced that this principle reveals a fundamental characteristic of nature. They are convinced that the fundamental processes of nature are not strictly determined. Something like free-will has to be put at the basis of natural phenomena. The older generation of physicists, including Einstein and Max Planck, think that Heisenberg's principle may be interpreted as a merely temporarily useful device.

The point at issue may be made clear as follows: We are accustomed to suppose that we can observe natural phenomena without disturbing them. By observing the motion of the moon, for instance, we do not disturb that motion. But when we come to single electrons the assumption is no longer justified. Unless an electron is interacting with the outer world it is, of course, in an unobservable condition. But an electron cannot interact with the rest of the world without at least one quantum of energy being involved. And the effect of this quantum, whether the electron gains it or loses it, is sufficient to disturb the electron in an unpredictable way. It is impossible, therefore, to deduce, from our present observations, the future behaviour of an electron. Thus a completely deterministic scheme for natural processes cannot be formulated. How are we to interpret this fact? It is perfectly possible, of course, to say that all natural processes are completely determined, but that this complete determinism eludes our methods of observation. But what is the use of postulating something that can never be verified? Why assume a hypothesis that can never be confirmed? An important principle of modern physics, first made explicit by Einstein, is that none but observable factors shall be imported into a scientific explanation. He objects, for instance, to Newton invoking absolute space in his explanation of centrifugal force, because absolute space is an entity which cannot be observed.

In the same way one may object to principles being invoked that can never be confirmed.

It may be that the upholders of the "free-will" theory are pleading for nothing more than the exercise of economy in constructing scientific hypotheses. If our methods of measurement are such that they cannot possibly reveal a deterministic universe then the fact that they do not reveal it is not, of course, a proof that it does not exist. But if we are necessarily limited to such methods what is the gain for science of assuming the existence of something they can never reveal? The universe we discover is conditioned, not only by what it is, but by our methods of approach.

A DISSERTATION ON NEWTON

Isaac Newton has been regarded, for the last two hundred years, as the dominant figure in the history of science. His law of gravitation has been regarded as the most perfect and universal of all scientific laws, and his discovery and exposition of it as the greatest single achievement of scientific genius. He has been, in the imaginations of many very able scientific men, an almost superhuman figure. It has been said, in our time, that Newton towers above all other scientific men to an extent which is without equal in any other branch of human achievement. Such an attitude, although it may be justified, seems to have a tendency to inhibit the critical faculties. The state of perpetual ecstatic admiration does not seem to be compatible with a genuine and penetrating attempt to understand the man and his achievements. The unsatisfactory character of most of the writings on Newton is partly due to the writers' attitude towards him, perfectly natural though that attitude may be. The fact, therefore, that the whole Newtonian outlook on the universe is now being replaced by a different one may enable us, as a psychological by-product, to get this colossal figure into some sort of perspective. It is unilluminating, for instance, to be told that Newton had the "perfect scientific mind." What sort of mind is that? How does it differ from the minds of Kepler and Cavendish, those two extremes of the "scientific mind"? And what was the quality of Newton's "originality"? How far was he the product of his time? And surely we could now endure a rather more acute discussion of his character as a man. We should like to know what that simple Christian piety, so greatly approved of by Sir David Brewster, really indicates in Newton. His curious reluctance to publish his researches, and his cheerful abandonment of science on being made Master of the Mint, are also matters of great psychological interest. So great a genius and fascinating a character deserves something more than exclamation marks. It is true that adequate studies of certain aspects of Newton's achievement have appeared; but we are still without a satisfactory critical biography of what was, presumably, the greatest of scientific geniuses.

One of the most interesting problems of Newton's character is presented by his attitude towards his own genius. His scientific capacity has probably never been equalled, and yet this "High Priest of Science," as Brewster calls him, certainly never took up a priestly attitude towards his science. He had none of that passion, verging on fanaticism, for scientific discovery that has distinguished so many scientific men. With unprecedented discoveries within his grasp, he would abandon an investigation for years, and turn his attention to other things. It almost seems as if some of his key discoveries were the result of a transient curiosity rather than of a passionate desire to explore the secrets of the universe. Once involved, his concentration was extraordinary, but, the particular point settled, he was as likely as not to drop the whole matter until some fresh burst of curiosity, or the entreaties of some unsuccessful investigator, made him take it up again. In this detached, almost indifferent, attitude towards his own powers, Newton is unique. It seems to be almost a matter of chance that he took up science at all. As a boy, Newton was largely occupied in making mechanical models, and he also, it is said, practised drawing and tried to write poetry. Unlike most great mathematicians, he gave no evidence of mathematical precocity. When he went to Cambridge, at the age of nineteen, it was not with any definite intention of studying mathematics. He came to mathematics through picking up a book on astrology at Stourbridge Fair and finding that he could not understand a certain diagram in it without a knowledge of trigonometry. He therefore purchased an English Euclid, but found it so easy that he threw it aside "as a trifling book." He went on to Descartes' Geometry, which was difficult enough to interest him, and from this to Vieta and Wallis's Arithmetic of Infinites. The new subject interested him considerably, and early in 1665, the year in which he took his B.A. degree, he had discovered the binomial theorem and invented the differential calculus. For part of this and the succeeding year, Newton lived at home to avoid the plague; and during this time, besides developing his calculus, he made various optical experiments, and thought out the fundamental principles of his theory of gravitation.

These really amazing achievements seem to have been attended with no sense of exultation. It is doubtful whether Newton was ever fully conscious of the difference between his powers and those of other men. Certainly he never betrays any sense of responsibility towards his genius. He spent a long lifetime in meditation, but chiefly because he found meditation a more

A DISSERTATION ON NEWTON

agreeable way than any other of passing his time. There is no trace of the conquering young heaven-stormer about the young Newton. His secretiveness seems to be, at bottom, the outcome of indifference. The motives that are supposed to inspire great discoverers, the desire to benefit their species and add to the sum of human knowledge, are almost as little discernible in Newton as in Cavendish. Having found that his optical researches aroused controversy, he writes:

> "I see I have made myself a slave to philosophy; but, if I get rid of Mr. Lucas's business, I will resolutely bid adieu to it eternally, excepting what I do for my private satisfaction, or leave to come out after me; for I see a man must either resolve to put out nothing new, or to become a slave to defend it."

These threats to withhold his results from the world, or even to abandon science altogether, were by no means empty threats. He did withhold many of his results for several years—indeed, it is doubtful whether, but for Halley's importunity, the "Principia" would ever have been written—and even before he became Master of the Mint he was on the point of abandoning science altogether. It would hardly be too much to say that whatever he did he did for his "private satisfaction." As a young man of twenty-six, after solving, at Collins's request, some problems that had proved insoluble to other mathematicians, he insisted that the results, if published, should be published without his name appearing, "for I see not what there is desirable in public esteem, were I able to acquire and maintain it: it would perhaps increase my acquaintance, the thing which I chiefly study to decline." The aloof, self-sufficient note here is quite unmistakable. And although he was often willing to assist other investigators, he never seems to have asked for help, nor to have invited collaboration. He regarded his contemporaries chiefly as men who might involve him in abhorrent controversies.

With no desire for "public esteem," with no sense of responsibility towards his genius, and with no feeling that he was called upon to "benefit humanity," there was not much to link Newton to his fellow-men. And, indeed, he never had an intimate friend and there is no evidence that he ever loved a woman. His manners have been described as pleasant and even charming; but, judging from a letter he wrote while still a young man, to a Mr. Aston who was about to travel, it would be possible to assume that they were largely diplomatic. He advises Mr. Aston, a young man of the same age as himself:

"When you come into any fresh company,
  1. Observe their humours.
  2. Suit your own carriage thereto, by which insinuation you will make their converse more free and open.
  3. Let your discourse be more in querys and doubtings than peremptory assertions or disputings, it being the designe of travellers to learne, not to teach. Besides, it will persuade your acquaintance that you have the greater esteem of them, and soe make them more ready to communicate what they know to you; whereas nothing sooner occasions disrespect and quarrels than peremptorinesse. You will find little or no advantage in seeming wiser, or much more ignorant than your company.

A DISSERTATION ON NEWTON

4. Seldom discommend any thing though never so bad, or doe it but moderately, lest you bee unexpectedly forced to an unhansom retraction. It is safer to commend any thing more than it deserves, than to discommend a thing soe much as it deserves; for commendations meet not soe often with oppositions, or, at least, are not usually soe ill resented by men that think otherwise, as discommendations; and you will insinuate into men's favour by nothing sooner than seeming to approve and commend what they like; but beware of doing it by a comparison."

The object of this kind of behaviour is to make the necessary intercourse with one's fellows as effortless as possible. These maxims are recipes for conserving energy and are proper, therefore, to the self-contained, meditative type. We can see that Newton's character admirably fitted him for the pursuit of scientific truth. He had not only greater abilities than his contemporaries, but a more "dispassionate" disposition. His most ardent rival, Robert Hooke, although often displaying an acumen scarcely inferior to that of Newton, was rendered comparatively ineffectual by his peevish temper and inordinate love of reputation.

Together with his fortunate moral and emotional qualities, Newton possessed a physical structure that could support the most intense and prolonged mental effort. His power of "paying attention," as he called it, was unprecedented. There are a number of well-known and authentic anecdotes that testify to his extraordinary power of concentration. He worked incessantly, often went without food and took very little sleep. He had no recreations or pastimes, and took no exercise. Nevertheless, he lived to the age of eighty-five. Humphrey Newton, who was his amanuensis during the time of the composition of the "Principia," states:

> "He never slept in ye daytime yt I ever perceived; I believe he grudged ye short time he spent in eating and sleeping ... In a morning he seemed to be as much refreshed with his few hours' sleep as though he had taken a whole night's rest. He kept neither dog nor cat in his chamber, whch made well for ye old woman, his bedmaker, she faring much ye better for it, for in a morning she has sometimes found both dinner and supper scarcely tasted of, whch ye old woman has very pleasantly and mumpingly gone away with."

Only once does he seem seriously to have broken down. There is evidence that he suffered during the years 1692 and 1693 from some form of mental derangement. The "Principia" was published in 1687, so that the tremendous effort of composing that work can hardly have been responsible for the breakdown. But that the breakdown occurred is made quite clear by the very queer letters he wrote to Pepys and Locke. In the letter to Pepys he says himself that he has "neither ate nor slept well this twelvemonth, nor have my former consistency of mind." Some authorities have thought that he never fully recovered from this illness, and in that way explain his subsequent scientific inactivity. But there is no reason to suppose that Newton had lost his powers. The challenge problems submitted to him in later years by Continental mathematicians were solved with the same old easy mastery. The fact is that to Newton one kind of activity was very much as

A DISSERTATION ON NEWTON

important as another, and he took his official duties as Master of the Mint very seriously. We need not suppose that the following remark, in a letter to Flamsteed, expressed a merely temporary mood: "I do not love to be printed on every occasion, much less to be dunned and teased by foreigners about mathematical things, or to be thought by our own people to be trifling away my time about them when I should be about the King's business." This is not the only occasion on which Newton refers to mathematical pursuits in a somewhat contemptuous tone. His general outlook appears to have been extremely conventional. He was a bigoted Whig and a bigoted Churchman. In these matters he gives no evidence of a profound, sceptical and independent mind. There can be no doubt that to Newton a great dignitary of Church or State was at least as important as a great scientific man; and he doubtless valued his position as Master of the Mint at least as highly as his position as President of the Royal Society. Perhaps we have another example here of his deep-rooted unconscious instinct for self-preservation. A sceptical outlook on religious and social matters would have disturbed his exquisite adjustment as a thinking machine. His general outlook we can interpret as an unconsciously formulated protective covering. Within its shelter he was able to pursue his proper business of dispassionate meditation.

We see, then, that Newton comes very near to Nietzsche's description of the "objective man," a passionless being concerned only to "reflect" such things as he is tuned to perceive. Newton is an even more singular example of this type than Cavendish; for Cavendish was at least devoted to science, while Newton seems to have been relatively passionless even about that. All these characteristics of Newton's must be considered as advantageous for the prosecution of his life's work. They were, all of them, necessary conditions for the perfect functioning of his intellect. And that intellect, as all the world has been long agreed, was probably the finest that has yet concerned itself with science. The impression his work makes on other scientific men may be typified by Laplace's remark that the "Principia" is the supreme manifestation of human genius, and by Lagrange's remark that he felt dazed at this exhibition of the capacity of the human mind. It is Newton's combination of mathematical power, insight into physical phenomena, and experimental ability, that makes him unique in the history of science.

Newton was about twenty-three years of age when he first surmised his law of gravitation; but he was hampered in his calculations by having assumed an incorrect value for the radius of the earth, and, as was entirely characteristic of him, he simply put the calculations on one side. Fourteen years later, Hooke, at the request of the Royal Scoeity, wrote to Newton asking if he had any contributions to send them, and received an answer that Newton had abandoned science. Newton was, as a matter of fact, devoting much of his time to theology, a subject that interested him all his life. But in his letter Hooke had mentioned Picard's new value for the radius of the earth. With these new data Newton took up his old calculations and verified, from the motion of the moon, his inverse square law. He also, having the orbits of the planets in mind, proved that, if a body describe an ellipse under the influence of a force directed to a focus, that force must vary as the inverse square of the

A DISSERTATION ON NEWTON

distance. And he further proved that a body projected under the influence of such a force would describe an ellipse or, more generally, a conic. Having obtained these enormously important results, Newton appears to have satisfied his curiosity for the time being, and put his calculations away—losing them, as it subsequently appeared. Five years later, in August, 1684, Halley came to Cambridge to consult Newton about a problem. Some of the acutest intellects of the time, as Huygens, Hooke, Halley, Wren, had a suspicion that the orbits of the planets pointed to the existence of a force directed towards the sun and varying inversely as the square of the distance. But, in spite of repeated attempts, they could not solve the mathematical problem involved. Wren, Hooke and Halley discussed the problem together; and Hooke, as was characteristic of him, professed to be able to solve it. In spite of the offer of a prize from Wren, however, he never produced the solution, and did not convince the others that he could. This was the state of affairs when Halley came to Newton and, without mentioning the speculations of Hooke, Wren and himself, asked Newton what orbit a body would describe under the action of the inverse square force. Newton immediately answered, *an ellipse.* "Struck with joy and amazement," Halley asked how he knew it; and then Newton, in looking for the calculation, found he had lost it. He promised, however, to repeat the calculation and to send it on. On receiving the demonstration, Halley went again to Cambridge. In the meantime, the conversation with Halley had aroused Newton's interest in the matter, with the result that, before the autumn, he had worked out many of the fundamental propositions of the "Principia." When

Halley saw these new results, he fully realized their immense importance, and prevailed upon Newton not only to send them to the Royal Society but really to devote himself to working out the consequences of his theory of gravitation. Thereupon, by an almost incredible intellectual effort, Newton composed the first book of the "Principia" by the summer of 1685. This feat has been called the greatest single illustration of Newton's powers, and it sets a standard of achievement for all time. By the summer of the next year the second book was completed, and the third begun. But Hooke's sleepless jealousy had been aroused by the communication of the first book, and he claimed to have preceded Newton in the discovery of the inverse square law. Newton dealt with his claims in some detail and then, after mentioning that he had designed the whole work to consist of three books, made the alarming statement:

> "The third I now design to suppress. Philosophy is such an impertinently litigious lady, that a man had as good be engaged in lawsuits, as have to do with her. I found it so formerly, and now I am no sooner come near her again, but she gives me warning."

Halley, who, to the great discredit of the Royal Society, had been left to bear the whole cost of printing and publishing the work, wrote an imploring letter to Newton and informed him that the Royal Society disallowed Hooke's claim. Satisfied on this point, Newton went on with the book, and added the almost unnecessarily handsome note, "The inverse law of gravity holds in all the celestial motions, as was discovered also independently by my countrymen Wren, Hooke and

A DISSERTATION ON NEWTON

Halley." The complete work, entitled *"Philosophiæ Naturalis Principia Mathematica,"* was published about midsummer of 1687. It made a great impression throughout Europe, and the whole edition was quickly sold.

It is the principles enunciated in this work that had dominated scientific thought for over two hundred years. Newton's other achievements are less important. His experimental work on light was of great value; but his corpuscular theory of light, although perhaps destined to a partial rehabilitation, proved itself much less satisfactory that the undulatory theory. Amongst his purely mathematical achievements the differential calculus, as it left his hands, suffered from an inconvenient notation. Although Newton was unquestionably the first inventor of this calculus, it is in the form given to it by Leibniz that it has proved best adapted to development. The spasmodic quality that we have noticed in following the history of the "Principia" is characteristic of much of Newton's scientific work. He would neglect the studies for which he was so superbly equipped in order to devote his time to theology and alchemy. He wrote on the prophetic books of the Bible, and devoted much study to the writings of Jacob Boehme. At one time he spent several months searching for the philosopher's stone. It is evident that Newton was credulous to an unexpected degree. He gives evidence of having possessed a strong vein of somewhat inferior mysticism. This has not been unusual with mathematicians, and it is only rarely that it rises, as in the case of Pascal, to a degree of insight that leads to real achievement. It is probable, therefore, that Newton's religious preoccupation arose partly from his love of abstract speculation and partly because it furnished an outlet for his mystical impulses. There is no reason to suppose that he had any real religious fervour, or that his piety was much more than passionless decorum.

The perfect "purity," as it were, of Newton's scientific mind is strikingly illustrated by his conception of the *rôle* of the scientific hypothesis.

"Hypotheses non fingo," he said on one occasion after being bitterly attacked by the followers of Descartes. But the word "hypothesis" here has not its meaning in modern science. The hypotheses to which Newton objected were of two kinds, metaphysical and physical. Descartes based the laws of nature upon certain axioms which he considered to be necessary truths. Newton insisted that all theories must be based upon the observation of phenomena, and consist in deductions from the phenomena. And he objected to his contemporaries' predilection for filling space with all kinds of aethers and fluids for which there was no evidence. His own theory of gravitation was not, in his mind, an hypothesis. He did not present it as explaining the mutual attraction of bodies for one another. He did not see that he was required to give such an explanation. What he had given was a mathematical description of the way bodies actually behaved. He did not profess to say *why* they behaved in that way. As a matter of fact, he did not think that science could give an answer to that question, since he thought gravitational action due to the direct activity of God. The Cartesians made the laws of nature embodiments, as it were, of *a priori* mathematical principles: that we could not verify them exactly was due to the imperfections of our instruments. Newton thought that all mathematical formulations of the laws of nature were probably imperfect. He believed that immutable and objective laws existed; but he believed that their mathematical formulation, even his own law of gravitation, would have to be modified as science progressed. The whole of this outlook, that seems so natural to us, was so peculiar to Newton that none of his contemporaries understood it. Nothing better illustrates his scientific quality than the fact that what is now regarded as the only correct scientific outlook should have been grasped by him alone.

Newton's dynamical system, which was until recently almost axiomatic in the minds of scientific men, resulted from the crystallization of the more or less confused ideas of his predecessors. Newton's first two laws of motion, for instance, and possibly also the third, can be deduced from Galilei's work; but they are nowhere enunciated distinctly. Newton's formulation and perfectly clear understanding of his dynamical system was a really very considerable feat—how considerable is shown by the fact that, twenty years after the publication of the "Principia," even Leibniz still had confused ideas on the subject. Newton was capable of overlooking a possibility, as when he thought the construction of an achromatic telescope impossible, but no one ever lived whose mind was less confused. This quality of perfect clarity which enabled him to formulate his laws and to seize the essentials of any problem, combined with the tremendous mathematical virtuosity that enabled him to apply his theorems so triumphantly, justified the contemporary opinion of him as "the lawgiver of the universe." The same quality made him dissatisfied with his early formulation of the calculus and, at a time when Leibniz remained content with "infinitesimals," there is evidence that Newton was working towards the subtle modern notion of the "limit." He was also one of the very few mathematicians of his time, and indeed, of the next hundred years, who realized that infinite series should be convergent.

The fundamental assumption of the Newtonian dynamics is the existence of one universal time system. He also assumed "absolute" space, but it is doubtful whether this assumption is really required by his system. The successful attack, by relativity theory, on the assumption of a universal time system has led to the creation of a new theory of gravitation and also makes the Newtonian law ambiguous. What Newton thought might possibly happen has happened. His law of gravitation has been replaced by a closer approximation. But Newton's law remains so close an approximation that it will doubtless continue to be used by astronomers for many years to come. The present condition of the scientific universe is somewhat chaotic. Everywhere there are difficulties, and one ingenious theory replaces another in the attempt to solve them. At the present time there is no one clear vantage point from which the whole of physical science may be surveyed. Our most inclusive theories cover a part only of the phenomena that have to be ordered. When Newton's work appeared men were persuaded that the key to the universe had been found, that this one man had made it possible for them to account for all phenomena and to banish all mysteries. We now know that this hope was illusory; and we may well doubt, from the standpoint of our greater knowledge and our disillusionment, whether another man will ever appear who shall occupy in the minds of men the position once held by Isaac Newton.

SCIENCE AND ART

J. B. S. HALDANE says somewhere that the universe is not only queerer than we suppose, but queerer than we can suppose. This sense of our inadequacy in face of the fundamental problems of existence seems to be at the basis of certain kinds of creative work. Its outward manifestation is a certain kind of originality. This kind of originality is very hard to define and yet, in the presence of it, we are immediately aware of it. The great creators whose work we have discussed all manifest this type of originality and, as we have suggested, it seems to be intimately connected with what is called mysticism. We feel that to minds of this temper the mystical experience is possible although it may not, as a matter of fact, ever have occurred. But the mystical experience is possible in the sense that certain fatal inhibitions are absent. Doubtless other qualities, emotional and so on, must co-exist with this mental temper before the mystical experience can become actual, but the attitude of mind is one for which the mystical experience is not impossible.

For some other types of mind we feel that mysticism must always be nonsense. Such types are "at home" in life in a way that a mind of a different type finds it hard to understand. They seem able, in some curiously bare and unrelated fashion, to accept the facts of experience as ultimate. They have so thoroughly accepted their assumptions that they are not even aware of them. Their "convictions," once acquired, whether they refer to moral judgments, legal codes, or even scientific theories, are henceforth without alternatives. Such men are often very energetic in practical affairs. They have an extraordinary capacity for taking the world as they find it. They master the lessons of experience very rapidly, so far as these lessons issue in devices for reaching their aims. And it appears very often that their success satisfies them, their type of success being accepted by them not only as sufficient justification for their outlook, but as the only possible justification for any outlook. This type of mind, although it can produce creative work of great value, never manifests the kind of originality with which we are here concerned. The attempts which have been made to explain "great men" as the products of their times find here their most plausible instances. Perhaps the majority of men everywhere belong to this type, although it is probable that their distinctive characteristics have received their clearest expression in Roman and modern Western civilization. Indeed, the chief justification for this attitude seems to be precisely its great survival value.

Yet the world has always been leavened by minds of the other type. Indeed, it would hardly be too much to say that all the greatest advances have come from minds possessed of this more general type of awareness. This is most obviously true of religion, and it is, perhaps, least apparent in science. Science is usually presented as something completely impersonal, as if its theories were inevitable products of the accumulated facts. The scientific mind is regarded as some sort of logical machine operating, in accordance with necessary and universal laws, on purely objective facts. In this it is distinguished sharply from works of art which are, it is admitted, very largely the result of personal idiosyncrasies. But the fact is that in certain scientific works, including some of the greatest, the personal element is very marked. It would be difficult to discover any individuality in, say, a catalogue of stars. And there are certain scientific theories which were such natural extensions of preceding ideas that their coming seems to have been inevitable. There are several such theories which have, in fact, been hit upon by two or more men at the same time. But Einstein has said of some of Gaus's work that if Gaus had not thought of it, it is difficult to believe that it would ever have been thought of. This may be said, also, of Einstein's most celebrated achievement, his theory of relativity. And Maxwell's electromagnetic theory, as we have already pointed out, was a very personal achievement. Such achievements are as individual as the greatest works of art. And we often find, with work of this quality, that the personal element exhibits that more general kind of awareness of which we have spoken.

This elusive quality that we have called "awareness" is, indeed, as apparent in science as in art. It is comparatively rare in either. And it cannot be said, if we judge by orthodox standards, that the greatest works in either sphere always exhibit it. It is not a criterion of "greatness." Herman Melville, for example, indubitably possessed a very unusual kind of awareness, but nobody could say that he was a greater writer than all his contemporaries who did not possess it. Again, it could not be said that Einstein is greater than Newton, although Einstein is certainly more "original."

It is the existence of this quality in a work of art that causes judgments about it to be so conflicting. If the work of art springs from a state of awareness akin to one's own, one is likely to attribute to it an altogether special value and significance. Other works of art, which one acknowledges to be greater, judged by all the canons, may be found relatively uninteresting. There are some people to whom a few bars of characteristic Beethoven mean more than a whole music-drama by Wagner. It is even possible, indeed, for a man to be a comparatively small artist and yet uniquely illuminating for certain people. Such extreme cases are not possible in science. The scientific audience is not so divided into groups. Yet the history of some scientific theories shows us that even a scientific theory can be opposed because it is found to be distasteful. Much of the opposition Einstein's theory encountered, for instance, was not founded on lack of experimental evidence or on logical flaws in its reasoning, but merely on the opponent's dislike for that kind of thing.

Since a scientific work can manifest "personality," in what essential respect is it different from a work of art? It might be said that the artist pursues beauty, whereas the man of science pursues truth. But this dichotomy only holds of certain extreme cases. A catalogue of stars, for example, may be said to embody nothing but truth, and there are some works of art, perhaps some musical compositions and some paintings, whose whole justification is their beauty. But there are many works of art, as is most obviously the case in literature, which also have a truth-serving function, and there are many scientific theories which are works of great beauty. The criteria of simplicity, economy, etc., employed in constructing a scientific theory are, at bottom, aesthetic criteria. If nature did not lend itself to these beautiful and harmonious constructions science would not be one of the major human activities. It would be reduced to a list of recipes and would be valued, like a catalogue or a time-table, for its practical usefulness. Both in his incentives and in his satisfactions the man of science is not essentially dissimilar to the artist. This is true of all sciences which have advanced beyond the stage of merely collecting data. It is most obviously true of the more general and abstract sciences, the mathematical sciences. It is particularly true of mathematics itself where, indeed, the distinction between art and science becomes so elusive that it can, with equal justice, be ranked as either.

MATHEMATICS AND CULTURE

IN talking about the relations of mathematics and culture, or, rather, about the cultural value of mathematics, I think it advisable that I should first say a little about what I think the word 'culture' to mean. In its general use it contains, I think, two ingredients, as it were. It refers to information and it refers to sensibility. An ignorant man, however refined his natural sensibilities may be, is not regarded to as cultured. And a man who has amassed an immense knowledge of facts, but is quite unable to distinguish between what is valuable and what is not valuable in his information, is not regarded as cultured. Of these two elements I am inclined to think that sensibility is the more important. What the old writers on aesthetics used to call taste is, I think, more important than knowledge for the formation of a cultured outlook. But the word 'taste' as they used it, is too narrow for our purposes. It refers to our aesthetic sensibilities, and doubtless the cultivation of these is a very important part of culture. We would agree, I suppose, that a man who is completely insensible to the arts cannot possibly be cultured. But an acquaintance with, and an appreciation of the arts, though necessary, is not sufficient. There are many other elements which enter into our ideal of culture. Thus I should say that a man with no historical sense, a man who took the particular conventions and ideas of his own time as the only ones worth respect, fell short of the ideal of culture. Mr. Henry Ford is reported to have said that "History is bunk." One can only conclude that, in one respect at least, Mr. Ford is uncultured. Similarly with an intense provincialism. The type of Englishman, who seems to have abounded in the nineteenth century, who regarded all foreigners as in all respects inferior, was what we should call uncultured. In fact, a good deal of what passed, and still passes, for patriotism, is probably only provincialism and therefore due to lack of culture.

Culture is chiefly, I think, the refinement and education of all our sensibilities including our intellectual and animal sensibilities, and not only those that are concerned with the arts. Other things being equal, I should say, for instance, that the man who could tell good wine from poor wine was more cultured than the man who could not. There is no need to labour this point. It would be generally agreed, I think, that an essential part of culture consists in the refinement and education of our sensibilities.

And now I come to my main subject. On what grounds can it be asserted that mathematics has a cultural influence? I gather, from various remarks I have come across in the writings of various authors, that mathematicians have sometimes been regarded as almost the least cultured of human beings. Mathematicians have sometimes been represented to us as being of so dry a nature and so warped a mind that almost every human interest is alien to them. Even James Clerk Maxwell, when a student at Cambridge, complained that some of the men there saw the whole universe in terms of quintics and quantics and seemed incapable of realising that the universe had other aspects. And we have all heard of the mathematician who, on being persuaded to read Milton's "Paradise Lost," said at the end that he didn't see what the man was trying to prove. Now it must be admitted that there are a good many mathematicians who lend colour to this assertion of insensitiveness. It seems to be possible for a man to have great mathematical ability and yet to be in other respects a barbarian. It would seem, in fact, that mathematics is a curiously isolated activity. It seems to be able to flourish in complete isolation from the rest of the elements of a man's nature. But we shall do well to distrust this conclusion. Psychologists are not disposed, now-a-days, to talk about isolated mental faculties. Indeed, some of them have gone to the other extreme, and deny the existence of any special abilities at all. A genius, according to them, is simply a man with an abnormal amount of general ability. What line his genius takes is dependent on his circumstances. I find it difficult to go as far as this. I find it difficult to believe that, if their circumstances had been interchanged, Napoleon would have composed the Ninth Symphony and Beethoven would have won the Battle of Austerlitz. But though I am disposed to think that there is a special mathematical ability I am not disposed to believe that it exists in a complete independence of everything else. I think we must admit, however, that it is more isolated than some other special abilities.

Nevertheless, can we claim for mathematics any general cultural influence?

Let us ask in the first place, what sort of information is given us by mathematics, and as this enquiry will tell us something about the nature of mathematics, I shall devote some time to it. At the beginning, when this mysterious activity was still young, it was supposed to give us the most valuable of all information. It was supposed to reveal to us the ultimate principles on which the universe is constructed. To the Pythagoreans every mathematical theorem had some mystic significance. Number, it was thought, is the very essence of the real. Other aspects of the real, which do not, at first sight, seem to have anything to do with number, were found by the Pythagoreans to be, after all, only aspects of number. The analogical method they used to establish this conclusion seems to us remarkably obscure. Thus they found that reason is merely an aspect of the number one, for the number one is unchangeable. To us the number one seems no more unchangeable than any other number. But the Pythagoreans must have thought there was a difference for they go on to say that the number two is indeterminate. "Opinion," therefore, as contrasted with reason, is the expression of the number two. Two is also, it appears, a feminine number, whereas three is a masculine number. Thus the very essence of marriage is expressed by the number five, for it is the sum of the first feminine and the first masculine number. This way of thinking seems very strange to us, but we can agree, I think, that it must have made the study of arithmetic a very exciting pursuit. We must remember that many good minds thought in this way, and that it is a way of thinking that persisted for several centuries. Indeed, I am not sure that it is even now altogether extinct. St. Augustine, for instance, found that God created the world in six days because six is the perfect number. The number six is perfect because it is the sum and also the product of the first three numbers. A number with such remarkable properties is obviously perfect. Michael Stifel, the great German algebraist of the sixteenth century, changed his faith because he found that the numbers corresponding to the letters making up the name of Pope Leo the Tenth added up to 666, the number of the beast in the Book of Revelation. This mathematician also, by applying a similar method to certain Biblical writings, found that the world was due to come to an end on October 3rd, 1533. Many peasants of his district, who believed him, abandoned their work, with the result that when the day came and passed, they found themselves ruined. This might surely be taken as an experimental proof that numbers did not possess the significance they were supposed to have. But the attitude persisted. Thus even Kepler, after demonstrating the mathematical properties of star-polygons and such-like figures, goes on to explain their magical properties in warding off diseases and other misfortunes. Indeed, Kepler's fundamental outlook was not unlike that of the Pythagoreans. He not only thought that nature obeyed mathematical laws, but he thought the reason for Nature's existence was that it illustrated these laws. This point of view is perhaps not unlike the philosophy of God the Pure Mathematician that Sir James Jeans has recently expounded to us. It would seem possible that Pythagoreanism still exists, not only in such beliefs as that thirteen is an unlucky number, but in more rarefied forms. In its lower forms it certainly still flourishes. Charles Dickens, you remember, was much impressed by the constancy of the yearly averages for deaths by railway accidents. If, by the end of November, he found that the figures were much behind, he was greatly depressed by the thought of the slaughter that was bound to take place the next month, and took care not to travel. Doubtless we have all met with several instances of the same thing. Another, and more respectable aspect of Pythagoreanism, is the doctrine that mathematics acquaint us with necessary truths.

The point of view is well put by Descartes in a famous passage from his Fifth Meditation:

"I imagine a triangle, though perhaps such a figure does not exist and has never existed anywhere in the world outside my thought. Nevertheless this figure has a certain nature or form or determinate essence which is immutable and eternal and which I have not invented and which depends in no way on my mind. This is evident from the fact that I am able to demonstrate various properties of this triangle, for instance, that its three interior angles are equal to two right angles, and that the greatest angle is subtended by the greatest side, and so on. Whether I want to or not, I recognise very clearly and evidently that these properties are in the triangle although I have never thought about them before and even if this is the first time I have imagined a triangle. Nevertheless, no one can say that I have invented or imagined them."

A triangle, therefore, according to Descartes, does not in any way depend on one's mind. It has an immutable and eternal existence quite apart from our knowledge of it. Its properties are discovered by our minds but do not in any way depend on them. This way of regarding geometrical entities lasted for two thousand years. To the Platonists geometrical propositions, expressing eternal truths, are concerned with the world of Platonic Ideas, a world apart, separate from the sensible world. The Platonic Ideas exist in a sort of heaven of their own and things on this earth are imperfect embodiments of them. To the followers of St. Augustine these Platonic Ideas became the Ideas of God; and to the followers of St. Thomas Aquinas they became aspects of the divine word. Throughout the whole of scholastic philosophy the necessary truth of geometrical propositions played an important part. If this outlook be justified, then the mathematical faculty gives us access, as it were, to an eternally existing, though not sensible world. Before the discovery of mathematics this world was unknown to us, but it nevertheless existed, and Pythagoras no more invented mathematics than Columbus invented America.

We no longer believe this to be a true description of the nature of mathematics. We no longer believe that mathematics is a body of knowledge about an existing, but super-sensible world. Some of us will be reminded of the claims certain theorists have made for music. Some musicians have been so impressed by the extraordinary feeling of inevitability given by certain musical works that they have declared that there must be a kind of heaven in which musical phrases already exist. The great musician discovers these phrases—he hears them, as it were. Inferior musicians hear them imperfectly; they give a confused and distorted rendering of the celestial reality. The faculty for grasping celestial music is rare. The faculty for grasping eternal triangles, on the other hand, seems to be possessed by all men.

These notions, as far as geometry is concerned, rest on the supposed necessity of Euclid's axioms. The fundamental postulates of Euclidean geometry were regarded, up to the early part of the nineteenth century, by practically every mathematician and philosopher, as necessities of thought. It was not only that Euclidean geometry was considered to be the geometry of existing space—it was the necessary geometry of any space. Yet it had quite early been realised that there was a fault in this apparently impeccable edifice. The well-known definition of parallel lines was not, it was felt, sufficiently obvious, and the Greek followers of Euclid made attempts to improve it. The Arabians, also, when they acquired the Greek mathematics, found the parallel axioms unsatisfactory. No one doubted that it was a necessary truth, but they thought there should be some way of deducing it from the other and simpler axioms of Euclid. With the spread of mathematics in Europe came a whole host of attempted demonstrations of the parallel axiom. Some of these were miracles of ingenuity, but it could be shown in every case that they rested on assumptions which were equivalent to accepting the parallel axiom itself. One of the most noteworthy of these investigations was that of the Jesuit priest Saccheri, whose treatise appeared early in the eighteenth century. Saccheri was an extremely able logician, too able to make unjustified assumptions. His method was to develop the consequences of denying Euclid's parallel axiom while retaining all the other axioms. In this way he expected to develop a geometry which should be self-contradictory, since he had no doubt that the parallel axiom was a necessary truth. But although Saccheri struggled very hard he did not succeed in contradicting himself. What he actually did was to lay the foundations of the first non-Euclidean geometry. But even so, and although d'Alembert was expressing the opinion of all the mathematicians of his time in declaring the parallel axiom to be the "scandal" of geometry, no one seems seriously to have doubted it. It appears that the first mathematician to realize that the parallel axiom could be denied and yet a perfectly self-consistent geometry constructed was Gauss. But Gauss quite realized how staggering, how shocking, a thing he had done, and was afraid to publish his researches. It was reserved for a Russian, Lobachewsky, and a Hungarian, Bolyai, to publish the first non-Euclidean geometry. It at once became obvious that Euclid's axioms were not necessities of thought, but something quite different, and that there was no reason to suppose that triangles had any celestial existence whatever.

We now believe that a mathematical theorem is necessary only in the sense that it is a logical consequence of its axioms and postulates, and that its axioms and postulates are arbitrary.

It appears, then, that there is no world, independent of the human mind, about which mathematics gives us any information. We can start from any set of axioms we please, provided they are consistent with themselves and one another, and work out the logical consequences of them. By doing so we create a branch of mathematics. The primary definitions and postulates are not given by experience, nor are they necessities of thought. The mathematician is entirely free, within the limits of his imagination, to construct what worlds he pleases. What he is to imagine is a matter for his own caprice; he is not thereby discovering the fundamental principles of the universe nor becoming acquainted with the ideas of God. If he can find, in experience, sets of entities which obey the same logical scheme as his mathematical entities, then he has applied his mathematics to the external world; he has created a branch of science.

Some writers, who accept this account of mathematics as a purely man-made thing, find it an extraordinary fact that the external universe, which is presumably not a man-made thing, should nevertheless obey mathematical laws. If mathematics is merely a mental game, like chess, why should the universe obey the rules of this game? This remarkable correspondence has led to far-reaching speculations. As a specimen of them I will quote from Sir James Jeans' recent book, *The Mysterious Universe*. He says: "A scientific study of the action of the universe has suggested a conclusion which may be summed up, though very crudely and quite inadequately, because we have no language at our command except that derived from our terrestrial concepts and experiences, in the statement that the universe appears to have been designed by a pure mathematician."

"This statement can hardly hope to escape challenge on two grounds. In the first place, it may be objected that we are merely moulding nature to our preconceived ideas. The musician, it will be said, may be so engrossed in music that he would contrive to interpret every piece of mechanism as a musical instrument; the habit of thinking of all intervals as musical intervals may be so ingrained in him that if he fell downstairs and bumped on stairs numbered 1, 5, 8 and 13 he would see music in his fall. In the same way, a cubist painter can see nothing but cubes in the indescribable richness of nature—and the unreality of his pictures shows how far he is from understanding nature; his cubist spectacles are mere blinkers which prevent his seeing more than a minute fraction of the great world around him. So, it may be suggested, the mathematician only sees nature through the mathematical blinkers he has fashioned for himself.

"A moment's reflection will show that this can hardly be the whole story. Our remote ancestors tried to interpret nature in terms of anthropomorphic concepts of their own creation and failed. The efforts of our nearer ancestors to interpret nature on engineering lines proved equally inadequate. Nature has refused to accommodate herself to either of these man-made moulds. On the other hand, our efforts to interpret nature in terms of the concepts of pure mathematics have, so far, proved brilliantly successful. It would now seem to be beyond dispute that in some way nature is more closely allied to the concepts of pure mathematics than to those of biology or engineering, and even if the mathematical interpretation is only a third man-made mould, it at least fits nature incomparably better than the two previously tried.

"Fifty years ago, when there was much discussion on the problems of communicating with Mars, it was desired to notify the supposed Martians that thinking beings existed on the planet Earth, but the difficulty was to find a language understood by both parties. The suggestion was made that the most suitable language was pure mathematics; it was proposed to light chains of bonfires in the Sahara, to form a diagram illustrating the famous theorem of Pythagoras, that the squares on the two smaller sides of a right-angled triangle are together equal to the square on the greatest side. To most of the inhabitants of Mars such signals would convey no meaning, but it was argued that mathematicians on Mars, if such existed, would surely recognise them as the handiwork of mathematicians on earth. In so doing, they would not be open to the reproach that they saw mathematics in everything. And so it is mutatis mutandis, with the signals from the outer world of reality, which are the shadows on the walls of the cave in which we are imprisoned. We have already considered with disfavour the possibility of the universe having been planned by a biologist or an engineer; from the intrinsic evidence of his creation, the great Architect of the universe now begins to appear as a pure mathematician.

"In the second place our statement may be challenged on the ground that there is no absolutely sharp line of demarcation between pure and applied mathematics. It would of course have proved nothing if nature had been found to act in accordance with the concepts of applied mathematics; these concepts were specially and deliberately designed by man to fit the workings of nature. And it may be objected that even our pure mathematics does not in actual fact represent a creation of our own minds so much as an effort, based on forgotten or subconscious memories, to understand the workings of nature. If so, it is not surprising to find that nature works according to the laws of pure mathematics. It cannot, of course, be denied that some of the concepts with which the pure mathematician works are taken direct from his experience of nature. An obvious instance is the concept of quantity, but this is so fundamental that it is difficult to imagine any scheme of nature from which it is entirely excluded. Other concepts borrow at least something from experience; for instance, multi-dimensional geometry, which clearly originated out of experience of the three dimensions of space. If, however, the more intricate concepts of pure mathematics have been transplanted from the workings of nature, they must have been buried very deep indeed in our subconscious minds. This very controversial possibility is one which cannot entirely be dismissed, but in any event it can hardly be disputed that nature and our conscious mathematical minds work according to the same laws. She does not model her behaviour, so to speak, on that forced on us by our whims and passions, or on that of our muscles and joints, but on that of our thinking minds. This remains true whether our minds impress their laws on nature or she impresses her laws on us, and provides a sufficient justification for thinking of the designer of the universe as a mathematician."

What are we to think of this argument? It seems to me that Sir James Jeans does not give sufficient weight to the two objections he imagines being brought against his theory. Both objections are serious. Some mathematicians assert, for example, that a mathematical web, as it were, can be woven about any universe containing several objects. If this be true then the only evidence for a mathematical designer of the universe is to be found in the fact that the universe contains several objects. This would seem to be very inadequate ground on which to arrive at so far-reaching a conclusion. The second objection has also been made. Mathematics or logic, it is stated, are merely devices of adaptation or accommodation to the world in which we find ourselves. They are ways of thinking that have been evolved in our struggle to survive. Our minds have been evolved to fit our circumstances, just as our bodies have.

In a different universe, supposing that life and consciousness could have existed, we would have evolved a different logic just as we would have evolved different bodies. I am not very happy with this point of view, but, until it is answered, I do not think we can conclude from the fact that we can understand the world the fact that it had a designer. And I would like to point out that it is not perfectly certain yet that we can understand the world. To say that the world obeys the laws of logic is to say that neither the world nor any part of it can be the subject of two true propositions which logic asserts to be inconsistent with each other. Well, even if the modern world does not violate this law the reader of modern atomic theory must sometimes feel that it is getting pretty near to doing so. When we are told, for example, that a light quantum is at one and the same time large enough to fill the object glass of a telescope and small enough to enter an atom, we may wonder what has happened to the law of contradiction. The apparent dilemma, we are told, points to a necessary revision of our notions of space and time. This means, I suppose, that a new mathematical web will be woven, and this supports the contention of the mathematical logicians that mathematics will always prove adequate to anything.

These remarks have been, perhaps, in the nature of a digression from my main subject. But before we can have a clear idea of the cultural value of mathematics we must know what it does for us, what its nature is. Is it a science? So far as we have gone it seems more like a game than anything else. And there is a school of continental mathematicians which asserts that this is what it is. Mathematics proper, they assert, is a sort of game, played with meaningless marks on paper, rather like noughts and crosses. They assert that mathematical analysis, as ordinarily taught, cannot be regarded as a body of truth, but is either false or at best a meaningless game. Not all mathematicians agree with this. There are some who still think that mathematics can be reduced to formal logic. I know of nothing more difficult than these attempts to pry into the nature of mathematics. And it is distressing to find, when one has reached the point of exhaustion, that the conclusions are still subject to controversy. So I shall leave on one side these fundamental investigations. I will merely remark, incidentally, that if mathematics is a game like noughts and crosses, its cultural value is presumably low.

But, raising the subject to a more superficial level, I will ask whether mathematics has not many of the characteristics of an art. In the first place I would point out that its history is not unlike that of an art, and particularly of the art of music. Like music, it seems to have an inherent power of development. We have all heard the remark that you only get out of a mathematical argument what you put into it, and it has always seemed to me that this remark is true only in a trivial sense. This remark was popularized by Thomas Henry Huxley, who was no mathematician, and who was engaged in a controversy at the time. I prefer a remark that I came across a little while ago, by Heinrich Hertz. He says:

"One cannot escape the feeling that these mathematical formulae have an independent existence and an intelligence of their own, that they are wiser than we are, wiser even than their discoverers, that we get more out of them than was originally put into them."

The history of mathematics seems to bear out this

suggestion. Doubtless many of the primary mathematical concepts have not been suggested by experience at all, but arose, quite without prevision, from the mathematical symbolism employed. Thus negative numbers were not suggested by experience. They arose automatically from the formula for subtraction, and they were so far from being foreseen that for a long time they were not understood. Even in the time of Newton, John Wallis, a very able mathematician, believed that negative numbers were greater than infinity. And for a long time the negative roots of equations were unintelligible to mathematicians. They simply neglected them. The mathematical machine had ground out these results, as it were, but they were so far from having been put into it that their emergence caused something like consternation. That is true, also, of imaginary numbers. When they first appeared no meaning could be attached to them. They were dismissed as meaningless products of the mathematical machine. There are innumerable instances of what we might call this self-generative power of mathematics. Thus mathematicians were led to invent algebraic equations of higher and higher orders purely from considerations of abstract form. Each equation suggested the next. It was not that nature was suggesting to them more and more complicated problems. The greater part of mathematics, in fact, has developed in accordance with an inner life of its own, although there are occasions, of course, where branches of analysis have arisen to meet the demands made by certain physical problems. On the whole, however, mathematics has been remarkably autonomous. In this respect it resembles the art of music more closely than any other art. Music is the least dependent on experience, on suggestions from the external world, of all the arts. Music owes practically nothing, for example, to the sounds that occur in nature. And the musician, except in the sort of music called programme music, is not concerned to describe or illustrate anything in external nature. Music, at least as much as mathematics, lives in a world of its own. Its development, also, has not been dissimilar. It has been a step by step development, not because, like a science, it has been accommodating itself more and more closely to an external world, but because primitive musical forms suggest more complicated forms. We see this in the development of counterpoint, and in the development of harmony, as well as in the development of such a great musical form as the sonata form. In both mathematics and music their independence of experience and their purely formal development, are distinguishing characteristics. If mathematics is an art, it is more like music than it is like any other art, and it may be suspected that it appeals to not dissimilar sensibilities. In this connection it is interesting to notice that many mathematicians have been musical. A statistical study would show, I think, that music is the favourite art of mathematicians. So far as I can judge, from a necessarily very imperfect knowledge, mathematicians are not often interested in painting, the art which is most dependent on the external world. Also, their literary taste, judging from the poetry they quote, is sometimes deplorable. But if they like music, they usually like good music. I have met only one mathematician, an artist in his mathematics, who was really indifferent to music. But he had a brother who was a very good musician.

Another point of resemblance between mathematics and music is the fact that they are the only two activities where we have the creative infant prodigy. The young Mozart and the young Pascal have not their like elsewhere. And this is what we should expect if Music and Mathematics are so largely independent of experience. The young mathematician and the young musician can proceed to create before they have learnt anything about the world because, as a matter of fact, there is nothing for them to learn.

One of the chief functions of an art is to give aesthetic pleasure, and before we decide that the cultural value of mathematics is that of an art, we must ask whether mathematics gives aesthetic pleasure. I do not think there is much difficulty about maintaining this. We all know, as a matter of fact, that mathematics has a very strong aesthetic aspect. Every mathematician feels the difference between an 'elegant' proof and a proof which, as Lord Rayleigh said, "merely commands assent." Everyone realises the difference between the mathematician who is an artist and the mathematician who is merely a workman. Many mathematicians have written about mathematics in a kind of prose poetry. Sylvester, who apparently saw all the colours of a sunset in a page of algebra, is a celebrated example, but I cannot forbear to quote a perhaps lesser-known example from Boltzmann, quoted by Max Planck in the recent Maxwell Commemoration Volume. Boltzmann is describing a paper by Maxwell on the Kinetic Theory of Gases. He says:

"At first are developed majestically the Variations of the Velocities, then from one side enter the Equations of State, from the other the Equations of

Motion in a Central Field; even higher sweeps the chaos of Formulae; suddenly are heard the four words "put $n=5$." The evil spirit V (the relative velocity of two molecules) vanishes and the dominating figure in the bass is suddenly silent; that which has seemed insuperable being overcome as by a magic stroke. There is no time to say why this or that substitution was made; who cannot sense this should lay the book aside, for Maxwell is no writer of programme music, who is obliged to set the explanation over the score. Result after result is given by the pliant formulae till, as unexpected climax, comes the Heat Equilibrium of a heavy gas; the curtain then drops."

We must admit, I think that, whatever we may think of Boltzmann's analogy, he is certainly expressing a strong aesthetic reaction. And it was Henri Poincaré, I think, who is reported to have said that in all his researches he had never been interested to find the value of x, but solely in the beauty of the methods by which he found that value. There is no need to multiply examples. Every mathematician knows that one of the chief charms, perhaps the chief charm, of mathematics, resides in its aesthetic aspect.

I conclude, therefore, that the cultural value of mathematics is that of an art, and that the art it most closely resembles is the art of music. The cultural value of music is to be found, I think, in the states of consciousness it awakes in us. A great piece of music makes us aware of feelings, of sensibilities, that perhaps we had never experienced before. A thousand shades of joy and sorrow, a refinement of ecstasy, a purity of desire, such as we have never yet known, can be evoked in us by music. Our inner life is enriched, and that is the only life worth enriching. And I claim for mathematics that it does a similar thing for the more intellectual part of the mind. It subtilises and refines our intellectual capacities as music refines our emotions. The student of mathematics passes continually from one level of abstraction to another. Such notions as the general conception of number, of a function, of continuity, really are additions to the resources of the mind. The student finds that ideas that were at first too elusive to be grasped gradually became permanent additions to his mental furniture. The man who lacks these resources, to whom these ideas are meaningless, does not realise the possibilities of the mind. He lives in a poorer world. He lacks certain sensibilities. To that extent he is uncultured. And if modern science persists with its present tendency of reducing the universe to mathematical relations between entities which are unimaginable, and can only be mathematically defined, of making the universe, in fact, a completely mathematical affair, then the non-mathematician will be completely at a loss. A fundamental department of knowledge will become completely inaccessible to him. He will be, in one very important respect, uncultured. Mathematics will then acquire a new cultural status. It will be valued for the part it plays in refining and educating certain mental sensibilities and also for the part it plays in providing the key to information which is indispensible to a truly cultured outlook. But even if it turns out that the universe is not essentially mathematical, that God is not, after all, a pure mathematician, it can still be maintained, I think, that mathematics is an essential part of culture.

SIR JOSIAH STAMP

SIR JOSIAH STAMP hesitated a little when I asked him what had been the dominant motive that had guided him in his choice of a career. "It would be difficult to answer that without appearing somewhat priggish, wouldn't it?" he said. He meditated for a few moments. "I can say, however," he went on, "that my life has not been consciously planned. I did not set out with the intention of doing what I have done. As a matter of fact, my earliest passion was for astronomy. Then I became immensely interested in Gothic architecture. I still like to think I know more about Gothic architecture than I know about anything else. Economics came to my attention because it was presented to me as a subject in an examination that I entered for. I discovered that I had a natural craving for this subject, and I went on with it. But it has been a step by step career. The day before I left the Civil Service I had no notion whatever that I was going to do so. There has been nothing planned about my career."

"What do you regard as the chief importance of the study of economics?"

"I think that our modern civilisation depends on it. At this particular moment our civilisation is, I believe, in danger. The only thing that can save it is right thinking about economics. Economics is *the* thing now. The crying need at the present time is for a great extension of this study. We want more first-rate minds to work out the science of the subject, and we also want a great number of popularisers who will impress the importance of these principles on the public. Unless this great effort of understanding is made, I think our economic society, which has recently become so much more complex, will be more than we have ideas to control. An effort should be made even if it means abstracting energy from other pursuits. Science, for instance, could, without disaster, remain where it is for another twenty years. We could get on with what we know. There is no real need for fresh scientific discoveries just now. But greater knowledge of economics is an international necessity."

"Do you think that mankind has progressed?"

"I think that mankind has progressed economically and spiritually. There is no longer the great gap that used to exist between the rich and the poor. I mean in essential matters. Of the things that the rich man has access to some only are really worth while. And the poor man has access to those things, the worth-while things, also. Society is, in this respect, more homogeneous than it ever was before. But there are disintegrating tendencies in society. To understand these we must come back to economics. The greatest influence tending to disintegrate society is the lack of a fixed standard of value. The fluctuations of money values are a real peril to society."

"Do you think that anything of a man, besides his influence and the memories of his friends, survives his bodily death?"

"You mean, do I believe in personal immortality? Yes; I certainly do."

"Do you think that there is scientific evidence for your belief?"

"No; I do not think that science has anything to say about it, one way or the other. But it seems to me that both philosophy and intuition are in favour of the doctrine of the immortality of the soul. A theory that conflicts with intuition or common sense has not much real power. When I was a student I thought that science involved determinism, and I could see no answer to the scientific arguments. In fact, I forced myself to believe in determinism, or, at any rate, I tried to. But my common sense rebelled against the theory. Although it seemed unanswerable I could not help feeling that it was all nonsense. It so outraged my common sense that I really *could not* believe it. Thus common sense saved me—as it so often does save people. Nowadays, of course, the doctrine of determinism has not the force it used to have, and through the fundamental ideas of physics itself it seems quite untenable. People's minds have been liberated by the new ideas that are abroad. The notion of the fourth dimension, for example, and the wide-spread interest in spiritualism, have revolutionised the mind and made an entirely new outlook possible."

"Do you regard the present system of rewards and discouragements as fair and desirable?"

"It has many great drawbacks, but economic rewards are, on the whole, given to those who fulfil economic wants. The men who make money do, on the whole, produce something that is wanted. I am not now saying whether the public *should* want these things. Indeed, I think we have got our sense of values lop-sided. There are various kinds of poverty. One instance of this is the way the Sabbath has been spoilt. The function of the Sabbath is to give man the opportunity of looking at quite different values from those that conditions his ordinary life. But we make our recreations the mere obverse of our occupations. Thus, if a man sits in an office all the week he wants to do the opposite—he wants to dash about in a motor-car—on the Sunday. But these two ways of employing his time really belong to the same class of values. One is merely the opposite of the other. Men require to realise that there are other values, quite outside this limited circle. I am referring to such things as poetry, philosophy, history, religion, beauty. And I suppose that great music can be ranked with these, although the music that people ordinarily listen to certainly cannot. We have little enough opportunity to cultivate these oases."

"Do you think that life on this planet has come about accidentally or do you think it is part of some great scheme?"

Sir Josiah was silent for some minutes. "What do you mean by an accident?" he said finally. "If I keep on throwing stones at a wall and one of the stones goes through a little hole and hits somebody on the other side, is that an accident? The chances of it doing so could have been calculated beforehand. Does science know of any accidents? Let us suppose that, ages ago, innumerable forces were let loose and, out of their combinations, our planet inevitably emerges. Is that an accident?"

"Let us take accident to mean absence of purpose. Do you think that purpose lies behind the appearance of life on this planet?"

"Yes, I think that something we could call purpose lies behind it all (regarding purpose as an order different from the order which would result from statistical probabilities at random), and I have to assume, therefore, that mind of some kind lies behind phenomena. Even the existence of all the millions of stars that cannot, apparently, support life, is no argument against purpose. It may have been a tremendous achievement, for all we know, to knock off our planet, and may have necessitated the whole material universe. Besides, those millions of stars may serve purposes of which we have no idea. We have only one idea of 'life'."

"Do you find the existence of suffering an objection to the idea of life being purposeful?"

"Well, suffering is sometimes beneficent. But not always. No, it sometimes appears quite gratuitous and evil, I agree. The existence of suffering is certainly a difficulty, but it does not, in my opinion, negate the notion of a fundamental purpose. We obviously cannot understand the scheme of things. It may be impossible to bring results about without suffering."

"Do you think it possible to reach any real assurance that a scheme of things exists?"

"Assurance, yes. But not proof—not mathematical and scientific proof. But I do not believe that mathematical proof is the only kind of proof. One can reach profound convictions through religious and artistic experiences. Such experiences conspire, it seems to me, to make one feel that there is a scheme. But this is not a conviction that one can demonstrate to others."

"Do you assume that the material universe exists quite independently of our consciousness?"

"Yes, certainly. I do not believe in the idealist philosophy. I believe that the universe revealed by science is an objective reality, and 'exists' quite independently of the human mind. As I have said,

I think that some form of consciousness existed before the human mind appeared. But it need not have existed. The universe would still be there."

"Do you think that the meaning of life, the justification of all human effort, is to be found in the future? Do we exist, in fact, to make the world better for coming generations?"

"Partly. But the individual life has rights of its own. I do not agree with the notion that our whole purpose is to serve the next generation. This is to find the meaning of life in a goal which perpetually recedes. But, also, I do not think we ought to be content with a purely personal development. Each individual's life is partly a means to an end and partly an end in itself."

"Do you think that selective breeding, as advocated by the eugenists, would help to bring about a better future race?"

"I think that positive eugenics is in its infancy. We have to find out, first of all, what human qualities are desirable before we apply ways and means of getting them. The matter is very complicated. What is intelligence, for example? There are various forms of it. And certain moral qualities are thought desirable by some people and undesirable by others. Is humanitarianism desirable, for example? Might it not be better in the long run biologically if we made ourselves hard and unsympathetic? All these questions must be cleared up before selective breeding is undertaken. There *is* no body of men, at present, fit to be trusted with the power of moulding the race."

SIR A. S. EDDINGTON

SIR A. S. EDDINGTON was disposed to think that his adoption of a scientific career was partially due to the fact that the way opened naturally. "If I had had difficulties to overcome I am not sure that I would have done so," he said, with a little smile. "My inner incentive? Well, I suppose that, as a youth, my chief incentive was curiosity. I was curious about the actual workings of Nature. I believe that is usually the chief motive with young scientific men. But as I get older I find I am more attracted by the aesthetic aspect of science. I am chiefly interested, now, in watching the scientific picture of the world unfold. As science advances it brings a new beauty and harmony into the scientific picture of the world and that, I find now, is the chief reward of scientific work."

"Do you agree with Einstein's remark that modern scientific speculations spring from a profound religious impulse?"

"I am afraid I cannot throw much light on that remark," he said slowly.

"The anti-materialistic attitude of religion would certainly be of advantage in modern science. It would help a man to see certain possibilities, to entertain certain speculations, which the old materialists, who regarded the universe as composed of little billiard balls, would have difficulty in grasping."

"Einstein, I believe, professes a strict determinism.

He believes that everything is predestined. Do you regard that as incompatible with his religious outlook?"

"No. But I do not agree with determinism. It seems to me contrary both to our intuitions and to scientific evidence. Everybody, in practice, has an intuition of free-will. We find it difficult to believe that all our future actions are, as it were, already written down. And in the latest theories of matter we have had to introduce a Principle of Indeterminacy. An electron does not seem to obey strictly determinate laws. We cannot predict exactly what it will do. And this does not seem to me to be a temporary difficulty due to our imperfect technique, but a revelation of an inherent characteristic of the universe. Of course, scientific determinism *may* come back. We cannot prove that it will not. But I see no reason to assume that it will. Determinism is opposed both to our intuitions and to the evidence. Why not drop it?"

"What do you consider to be the general humanistic importance of science?"

"Er—could you make your question more precise?"

"Well, some people find the justification of science in its practical applications. The arts are not justified in that way. Do you consider that the true justification of science is something analogous to the justification of the arts?"

"We must first decide what we suppose the human race to be aiming at. I cannot believe that human beings exist simply in order to breed more millions of human beings. The human race must be aiming, in some way, at becoming finer. Science and art are justified to the extent to which they contribute to that aim. Of course, if you are asking for money for scientific research, then stress the practical side of science. But that is not the true justification of science. I believe that science, like art, enables mankind to approach nearer to the realisation of the absolute values that alone give an aim and meaning to life."

"Then you believe in absolute values?"

"I think we all do, in practice."

"So that a life wholly devoted to science would not seem to you an incomplete life? You do not share the Greek ideal of the perfectly balanced life?"

"I think we want different types of men, but I am not keen on the notion of the perfectly-balanced human being. We don't want a race of Isaac Newtons, but I consider that Isaac Newton's life was a good life. I think a man should have other interests, but chiefly because they refresh him and enable him to devote himself to his main preoccupation with greater keenness and power. A life spent in complete devotion to an absolute value is a good life."

"Then when the human race completely realises these values it will have reached perfection?"

"I don't think that a static perfection is to be desired. Life must be dynamic. It may be, for example, that the human race is no better now than it was two thousand years ago. But it is different, and that in itself is a good thing. If the human race ever achieved a static perfection, it would be time for it to come to an end, for there would be no possibility of further achievement, and therefore there would be nothing to live for."

"Do you think that life on this planet is the result of some kind of accident, or do you think it is part of a scheme?"

SIR A. S. EDDINGTON

"I think it quite possible that life, as a physical phenomenon, has come about by accident. I do not find, in myself, any bias against the idea that life arises naturally from certain physical aggregates. That may even be demonstrated, some day, experimentally. But consciousness seems to me to be on an entirely different plane. Consciousness is fundamental. It must already be assumed in all discussions about the origin and nature of anything. The material universe itself is an interpretation of certain symbols presented to consciousness. When we speak of the existence of the material universe we are presupposing consciousness. It is meaningless to speak of the existence of anything except as being connected with the web of our consciousness."

"Yet, according to astronomical and geological theories, there was a past existence of the earth before consciousness appeared on it. Did not the earth then really exist?"

"What do you mean by reality? We use the word in at least two senses which I have described in my book as 'reality' and 'reality' (loud cheers). The past reality of the earth is real to me in so far as it is connected to the web of my consciousness. I do not think we understand what we mean by 'existence.' The notion of past existence, before consciousness appeared, is a very elusive idea. We must remember that the notion of time, as it occurs in science, is a mere abstraction. The notion of time is, I believe, an abstraction from the dynamic nature of consciousness. Consciousness is essentially dynamic, and the 'time' of science is a most imperfect representation of this quality."

"Do you believe that anything of a man, besides his

influence and the memories of his friends, survives bodily death?"

"I would really prefer not to discuss that question. I have nothing to say for or against survival from a scientific standpoint."

"What do you think of the distribution of rewards, fame, money, and so on, in the modern world? Do you think they tend to encourage the finest achievements?"

"I think that publicity is bad for science in some ways and good in others. One wishes to spread scientific knowledge and the scientific spirit as widely as possible, and to satisfy the many among the public who are keenly interested in developments of science. But it is not always a good thing for science itself. There are certain kinds of scientific work, of the greatest importance and value to science itself, which cannot possibly be represented to the public. Such work has no publicity value and the public knows nothing about it. If science is made to depend to any extent on its publicity value, the tendency will be for such work to be neglected. Men will tend to concentrate on the 'showy' work in science. That would be a very undesirable state of affairs. I also think that the level of material rewards for scientific work should not be made too high. We do not want them to be so high that they attract men to science merely as a profitable career."

"But would such men be successful in science?"

"I am referring to able men who are not really keen on science. Such men could very well do sufficient work in science to ensure for themselves a comfortable position. And, having achieved that, they would probably not trouble themselves any further if they were not keen on science for its own sake. It would be impossible to get rid of them. And yet they would be keeping out really keen men. A scientific man wants his material circumstances to be reasonably secure, of course. But I do not think he should ask for more than that."

"And what about the distribution of rewards in the world outside science? For instance, the newspaper boosting of mediocrities, the sham reputations, and so on. Does that annoy you?"

"I'm afraid that is not my subject," said the Professor, smiling. "I suppose my reaction to that sort of thing is very much the reaction of any other educated person. I suppose it *is* annoying, in a way. But no, I'm afraid I don't think much about it."

SIR J. H. JEANS

"My early bent," said Sir J. H. Jeans, "was towards the practical and the concrete. At school I first of all took the classical side, but this left me dissatisfied. It seemed to me somehow unreal. I then found I was more interested in mathematics, and went over to the mathematical side. But that, also, seemed somewhat unreal. My desire, at that time, was to be an engineer. I used to amuse myself by making electric light in my bedroom and by experimenting with chemicals. Finally, I found what really satisfied me in science. I suppose mere curiosity was one of my guiding motives; another was the delight of controlling nature—as in those youthful experiments. Now, of course, I prefer abstractions."

"For their aesthetic aspects?"

"Well, yes, very largely. Undoubtedly the aesthetic element is one of the great attractions of the mathematical sciences. For that reason the mathematician does not feel satisfied with a proof until it is 'elegant.' And I think the desire to write well is another manifestation of the same thing. No; I do not think that the aesthetic element is equally prominent in all the sciences. I do not think it plays much part in, for example, chemistry and physiology. In my scientific reading, I have noticed that mathematical papers are usually better written than those dealing with other sciences. Physiologists and chemists seem to me more often to be content just to get at the facts."

SIR J. H. JEANS

"What do you think is the real importance of science to mankind?"

"I think that a *sufficient* justification for science can be found in its practical applications. Its usefulness in diminishing disease and in other ways enabling men to live fuller lives is sufficient, in itself, to justify all the labours of scientific men. But it does, in addition, aid understanding, and that, to my mind, is its primary importance. Man's desire to understand, just for the sheer joy of understanding, is one of the marks that differentiate him from the animal.

"A life devoted to understanding nature does not require any external or utilitarian justification. The Greek ideal of a perfectly balanced life is possibly a good ideal for the average man, but not, I think, for any man with very special aptitudes. For instance, I do not see why a man with extraordinary talents for science, art or music, should be expected to devote any large part of his peculiarly valuable energies to other ends. It would surely have been a loss if Newton had devoted some of his time to being a parish councillor? I regret, however, that he did not have children. It is unfortunate, I think, that so many first-rate scientific men have died childless. And I think this because I believe there is sufficient evidence to show that the children of exceptional parents are above the average."

"Do you believe that mankind is progressing?"

"The question assumes that progress is one-dimensional—that there is some one definite line of progress. I do not believe this. I do not think that the human race, as a whole, can be said to be up to anything in particular. The only objective that all human beings seem to have in common is pleasure. Apart from that it is impossible, it seems to me, to discover any common aim. There are too many countervailing forces for any definite direction to emerge. In certain directions there has been indubitable progress. For instance, there has been a real growth in the social conscience. Witch-burning would be impossible to-day. On the other hand, it is still possible, I suppose, for men to be systematically persecuted on grounds which are just as irrational. Yet, on the whole, I am sure that in this direction we have progressed. But, to consider another direction, I think that the present day democratic influence is definitely bad. I am not urging, of course, that the ordinary man's happiness and comfort should be neglected. But I think that altogether too much attention is paid to the opinions of the uneducated man, especially where these conflict with the knowledge of experts. Besides defeating its own ends, this leads to a vulgarisation of thought and feeling."

"Do you believe that life on this planet is the result of some sort of accident, or do you believe that it is part of some great scheme?"

"I incline to the idealistic theory that consciousness is fundamental, and that the material universe is derivative from consciousness, not consciousness from the material universe. If this is so, then it would appear to follow that there is a general scheme. My inclination towards idealism is the outcome largely of modern scientific theories—for instance, the principle of indeterminacy may provide an escape from the old scientific doctrine that nature is governed by strictly deterministic laws. In general the universe seems to me to be nearer to a great thought than to a great machine. It may well be, it seems to me, that each individual consciousness ought to be compared to a brain-cell in a universal mind."

"Do you think that the existence of suffering presents an obstacle to belief in a universal scheme?"

"No, I think it possible that suffering can be accounted for along the usual ethical lines. That is to say, evil may be necessary for the manifestation of greater good, just as danger is necessary for the manifestation of courage."

"But does not suffering, in many cases, seem to be entirely pointless—to lead to no good that we can see?"

"I agree that we cannot understand the scheme of life—if there is one. At present we understand hardly anything. I hold, very strongly, that our present knowledge, in comparison with what man's knowledge may become, is merely infantile. In fact, on all these questions my philosophy could be summarized by the unpopular phrase, 'Wait and See.'"

"Do you think that anything of a man besides his influence and the memories of his friends, survives bodily death?"

"If we regard our individual minds as component parts of a universal mind, your question needs to be stated in a different form. But, apart from that, the problem is full of difficulties. The notion of time is involved. How are we to regard time—especially in view of relativity theory? You probably remember the remark attributed to Hermann Weyl that 'events do not happen; we come across them.' And the fact that we all come across them at the same moment is surely significant. It rather strengthens, don't you think, the notion that we are all parts of a general mind?"

"Do you agree with Einstein's remark that modern scientific speculations spring from a profound religious impulse?"

"I agree with that remark if the word religious be sufficiently widely interpreted. I think that the greatest achievements generally spring from what may be called a religious impulse. An obvious case of this is provided by fifteenth-century Italian art, which certainly seems to me greater than the secular art that succeeded it. And in science I think that the best work is that which is undertaken purely for the truth's sake, or undertaken wholly for the benefit of humanity. I suppose one could describe both these motives as religious impulses."

"Do you think that the distribution of rewards in the modern world is likely to encourage the best in men? What, for instance, do you think about the millionaire pork-butcher?"

"There is obviously much that is wrong with our modern society. But I do not think that much is to be gained merely by trying artificially to alter the distribution of rewards. History shows that *someone* will always contrive to get an unfair share. But there is, I think, a far greater evil than the infrequent millionaire pork-butcher, who at least finds employment for thousands of men, and provides cheap pork for millions more. I am thinking of the frequent and ever increasing type of being, who enjoys all the benefits of civilisation without contributing anything at all."

"Could not these people be educated in finer ideals?"

"Some of them, perhaps. But there are many men

who cannot be educated to fineness. It would be better to breed them out."

"Don't you think that much might be lost by selective breeding? Consider, for example, epilepsy. I believe that both Dostoevsky and Mahomet were epileptics."

"You have to go rather far afield for your two examples," said Sir James, smiling. "But I would willingly run the risk of losing a few geniuses if I could breed out epilepsy. The *average* epileptic is certainly lower than the average normal person. In discussing selective breeding we must, at the moment, be content with averages. Individual cases cannot upset a generalisation based on averages. For instance, you may be able to give instances of remarkable men who are not mentioned in 'Who's Who.' They may even be more remarkable than those who *are* mentioned in 'Who's Who.' But you could not maintain that the *average* of all those who are not mentioned is as high as the average of those who are mentioned. In the present state of eugenics we must be content with such somewhat rough-and-ready averages. But, even so, I think there is a good case for selective breeding."

"I gather that you are not a believer in democracy?"

"I think that democracy, in the abstract, is bad. But then I also think that the present alternatives to democracy are bad."

"Then what is your solution?"

"I think we may reasonably anticipate that the development of the social conscience will in time give rise to a class which will be generally recognised as natural leaders and trusted as such."

"Like H. G. Wells's *Samurai?*"

"I have not read the book. But now that our conversation is at an end, I would like to add a concluding remark, to which I attach some importance. And that is that I do not think I have the right to give a definite opinion on any of the questions that we have discussed this afternoon."

M. PAINLEVÉ

PAINLEVÉ, of course, was more concerned with problems in pure mathematics than with the problems of physical science, and many devotees of pure mathematics seem to regard it as one of the greatest of the arts. It is not surprising, therefore, that Painlevé should have stated that his guiding motive has been purely aesthetic.

"The mathematical passion is an aesthetic passion," he declared emphatically. "I consider myself to be an artist. My motives have been those of any other artist with a passion for beauty. But this passion has been by no means exclusively directed towards mathematics. The mathematical passion seized upon me when I was only nine years of age. I studied with such intensity that I had reached the degree standard in mathematics by the time I was eleven. I was not a mere specialist, however, exercising an isolated faculty. I also made brilliant studies in the classics and in literature, and my passion for these subjects was quite as great as my passion for mathematics. But although all these subjects seemed to me, then, of equal importance, my teacher was not deceived. He told my father that, in spite of my interest in literature and the classics, I must nevertheless be a mathematician. But in those days the beauty of mathematics and the beauty of literature moved me equally. I remember weeping, through excess of aesthetic delight, twice on the same day—

sometime in my fifteenth year. The first occasion was produced by the description of the parting of Hector and Andromache, and the second was produced by the definition of acceleration given by Newton. Mathematics is still, to me, an aesthetic passion. I am at this moment in the middle of a short holiday. I am spending that holiday working out the mathematical theory of the gyroscope."

"Do you think that the guiding motive in constructing theories in physical science is also aesthetic?"

"Not altogether. The drive towards beauty in physical science is trustworthy only up to a point. A scientific theory must, of course, be constructed in accordance with the laws of our own mind, and yet it must be adapted to events in the external world. The scientific theorist is in the position of a man making clothes for a body he does not see. His measurements only enable him to say that the garment fits the body at certain points. The actual shape in which he fashions the garments depends on these points of contact, and also on his own aesthetic preferences. As science is successful, there must be a correlation, I think, between our consciousness and external events. The two things cannot be completely independent of one another."

"How far does this correspondence go? We, for instance, have an intuition of free-will, whereas the external universe has been presented by science as being a completely deterministic scheme. But the new principle of indeterminacy states that the fundamental processes of nature are *not* completely determined. What do you think of that principle?"

"I regard it merely as a temporarily useful hypothesis to help us over certain difficulties. I do not regard it as a discovery about the nature of the universe. I do not believe that there is anything like free-will at the basis of material phenomena. The Principle of Indeterminacy is only an expression of our present ignorance. Science will come back to determinism."

"Do you think that mankind has progressed?"

"Yes, in material matters."

"And morally?"

"Ah, that is a different question. What do we mean by moral progress? Is there one universally accepted standard of morality? What, for instance, would the Chinese or the Brahmins think of our present state of civilisation? I can hardly suppose that they would think we had progressed morally. It is evident that different peoples have different concepts of morality. And yet I believe that certain fundamental moral principles can be discovered. All systems of morality accept certain fundamental values, just as certain principles are obeyed by a geometry, however crude. A primitive people might invent a very primitive and imperfect system of geometry, but there are certain fundamental principles that would be embodied in that geometry. I think the same holds good of moral systems, however imperfect."

"What are these fundamental moral principles?"

"I think there are two main ones—justice, and respect for human life. I think that every system of morality assumes that these are fundamental values. We could measure moral progress by the extent to which these principles are observed."

"Then, on that basis, do you think we have progressed morally?"

"Not individually. But I think that perhaps a collective progress has taken place. Perhaps nations as a whole are more just and have more respect for human life. The individual man has not altered."

"What do you think of the present state of society—of its rewards and discouragements?"

Painlevé replied with great vigour.

"I think that the present social system is perfectly barbarous. The rewards bestowed by modern society bear no relation to the real value of the achievements that are thus rewarded. The disparity is particularly obvious when we consider the rewards given to scientific work. Everything in modern civilisation depends upon science, and yet the standing of science in a modern community is very far from being commensurate with its importance. But I do not think this state of things will last. We shall be forced to pay adequate attention to the really important things—particularly science. We shall be forced to do this in mere self-defence. A society ignores science at its peril. Yes, I think things will get better, always providing that Europe preserves a peaceful course. (He shrugged his shoulders.) And that is doubtful."

MR. ALDOUS HUXLEY

"My chief motive in writing," said Mr. Aldous Huxley, "has been the desire to express a point of view. Or, rather, the desire to clarify a point of view to myself. I do not write for my readers; in fact, I don't like thinking about my readers. In addition, I like writing for writing's sake. I am conscious of possessing a certain talent, and I like to exercise it in solving the literary problems I put to myself. But this aspect of my work interests me less than it did. I am chiefly interested in making clear a certain outlook on life."

"How would you describe that outlook?"

"Well, I cannot say that I have yet reached a definite outlook. My books represent different stages in my progress towards such an outlook. Each book is an attempt to make things clear to myself so far as I had gone at the time it was written. In that sense they are all provisional."

"Why not wait until your outlook is mature before writing about it?"

"Well, I must make money in the meantime. That is not the whole reason why I publish, of course, but it is certainly a real and important one. Although I write for myself and not for my readers, I must have readers in order to get a living."

"What do you think is the general humanistic importance of your work?"

"I think it is important as an element in a more

general outlook. I believe that mankind is working towards some definitive and comprehensive outlook on the world, and I regard my work as contributing something towards that. I think it possible that some of the very great men of the past had achieved a really comprehensive outlook, but that fact does not make the work of lesser men like myself unnecessary. For an outlook must be *realised*, not only learned. A man must go through the various stages for himself. We cannot profit by another's conclusions unless our own experiences are similar. My outlook is the result of my temperament and training. My attempts to make that outlook clear may be useful to people who are like myself. There are things I have written that I would now modify if I could. They do not fit in, I see, now, with the outlook I am developing."

"And why do you think it important to help forward a clear general outlook?"

"Because I think that clarity of outlook is a good thing in itself. It does not require to be justified by practical or other considerations. Clarity is intrinsically a good thing. It is worth aiming at purely for its own sake. As I said, my dominant motive in writing is to make things clear to myself, and my writing is important to others in so far as it helps them to become clearer."

"Do you think that mankind has progressed?"

"Yes, since Neanderthal times. But it is very difficult to say that mankind is now progressing. The question is, What do we want to aim at? Progress in one direction hinders progress in some other direction. For instance, our great mechanical progress has hindered intellectual progress. And it seems clear to me that intellectual development often hinders emotional development. If we evolved a race of Isaac Newtons that would not be progress. For the price Newton had to pay for being a supreme intellect was that he was incapable of friendship, love, fatherhood, and many other desirable things. As a man he was a failure; as a monster he was superb. I admit that mathematical science is a good thing. But an excessive devotion to it is a bad thing. Excessive, or rather exclusive, devotion to anything is bad."

"So you do not admire saints?"

"No. I think the right ideal is the Greek ideal. A man should cultivate a balance and harmony amongst all his powers. He should not sacrifice any of his instincts and desires to others. They all have their rights to expression."

"But surely you think that some desires are intrinsically better than others? Would you say, for instance, that, in order to be complete, a man ought to be a bit of a dipsomaniac as well as a bit of a mathematician?"

"I see nothing inherently wrong in dipsomania. Surely the only reason why we disapprove of a man being a dipsomaniac is because it prevents his being anything else?"

"And you disapprove of Newton on the same grounds?"

"Yes. But I rank Newton above a dipsomaniac because his work did not end with himself. It influenced the future, and was therefore valuable. We cannot say that anything whatever is good unless it refers to the future. All values are purely human. Nothing can be good or bad if the human race comes to an end. I am afraid all this sounds rather silly. After all, I am not *sure* that our notions of good are purely human. There are some experiences which produce in us a curious feeling of ecstasy which seems to give them some special significance. But I don't know what that significance may be."

"Do you think that life on this planet is an accident or do you think it is part of some great scheme?"

"I would much prefer to believe that there is a general scheme of things, but I know of no evidence for it.

"But the mere fact that men would prefer to believe that a scheme exists may be an indication that a scheme does exist. It seems strange that there should be a universal and powerful desire which is doomed to non-fulfilment. Also, the existence of suffering would seem to necessitate some great scheme for its explanation. Suffering seems to me at present quite inexplicable. I have read no explanation of it that seems to me at all plausible. Of all the explanations that have been offered I find the Indian notion of Karma the most satisfactory. I mean the notion that our past lives condition our present life—that we have made ourselves what we are. But the Indians suppose that the final end of the whole thing is Nirvana, and that prospect does not seem to me very pleasing. No, I am afraid there is no solution. Evil is an absolute thing. It is not an aspect of good. It cannot be explained away. If there is a scheme I think it must be something of which we would approve. That is to say, if there is a universal mind, I do not think it can be indifferent to human values and aspirations. It must be a mind something like ours. And I expect the whole problem arises because of our undeveloped consciousness. Very likely the problem does not really exist at all. It is a pseudo-problem, and originates merely from the way we think about things. Of course, if there is a scheme of things, something that we could call ultimate reality, then it is possible that our values, that I have called purely human, really refer to this reality. But I confess that I am a pragmatist by temperament. My tendency is to believe that everything is purely human, and that nothing in our experience points beyond itself to some ultimate reality."

"Do you believe that anything of a man, besides his influence and the memories of his friends, survives bodily death?"

"I don't believe that a man's personality survives his death, but I think there is very good evidence that something survives. I don't think that all the results claimed for psychical research are to be pooh-poohed. I am quite convinced, for example, that telepathy exists. I have had personal experiences of telepathy which entirely convince me."

"What is the 'something' that you think survives death?"

"I don't know how to describe it. But I think that various psychic experiments prove that something survives that possesses memory, at any rate. It may not be a complete personality. It may be something that reverts to a common mind. C. D. Broad's theory of a 'psychic factor' seems to be, from what I have heard of it, the sort of idea I have in mind. He supposes that there is something he calls a 'psychic factor.' It is not a mind. It is something which, in combination with a physical brain, forms a mind. When the psychic factor of a deceased person forms a temporary connection with the physical brain of some living medium it forms a temporary mind having the memories that belonged to the deceased person. This is not, perhaps, a very cheerful doctrine. It gives no room for the future development of a human personality after death, and therefore does nothing to alleviate the problem of suffering. But I think some such idea is necessitated by the psychic experiments."

"Do you think that the present state of civilisation, with its standards of rewards—fame, money, etc.—encourages the best in men?"

"Do the best men have the most money, in fact? Well, it is obvious that they don't. But would it be a good thing for them if they had? I doubt if a modern Isaiah would be benefited by being made a millionaire. The poverty and tribulation the world metes out to such men is probably the best reward it could offer them. Riches and honours would probably stultify them. Nevertheless, I do not claim for one moment that the modern system of rewards is sensibly designed. Think of Channel swimmers? Fancy bestowing fame on a man for swimming the Channel! It is surely obvious that modern reputations are largely due to the general *bêtise latente*.

"I believe that there is more vocal silliness in our age than there ever was before. Consider our popular newspapers. It is evident that they exist merely in order to stupefy the public. Even politics is supposed to require too much intelligence, so they leave out politics. And I believe that things will grow worse. We can sink to an even lower level, as we see in the case of the American Press. But there will be a revolt. The people are eager for some kind of religion. The community singing in this country and the religious ceremonies in Hollywood

Bowl in America are instances of this. The next revolution will not be economic; it will be psychological. And the revolution will occur because of the intolerable nature of the standardised lives we live. All civilised peoples are suffering from a terrible boredom.

"This is largely due to the fact that everybody is passive nowadays. People no longer create their own amusements. They endure them, they suffer them. The piano trade, for example, is declining, but the gramophone trade is going up. And it is a psychological fact that the more things we acquire the less satisfaction they give us. Half the things that people require nowadays are not really wanted by anybody. The desire for them is created wholly by advertisement. Electric cigar-lighters, for instance. Who really wants an electric cigar-lighter? I cannot understand these things. And another thing I cannot understand is the amazing craving of all classes of people for newspaper celebrity. It is not as if they took newspaper reputations seriously. They are quite cynical about them. But they have an overpowering desire to see their names in the newspapers. It is all very strange."

PROFESSOR MAX PLANCK

PROFESSOR MAX PLANCK has recently been appointed Director of the Kaiser Wilhelm Gesellschaft, at Berlin; but his position in the world of science is not to be measured by such academic distinctions, exalted as they may be. For there must always be a Director of the Kaiser Wilhelm Gesellschaft, whereas, Planck is one of the few truly original minds of his time, creator of the revolutionary and immensely important Quantum Theory. This theory, together with Einstein's Relativity Theory, covers practically the whole of modern physics. It would hardly be too much to say that the major part of the work now being done in theoretical physics proceeds on the basis of ideas which have grown from those originally supplied by Planck thirty years ago.

In my interview with him Professor Planck replied to all my questions with a quite remarkable lack of hesitation. It would seem that his ideas on these subjects are now definitely formed, or else that he thinks with remarkable rapidity—probably both suppositions are true.

"My incentive in studying science," he said, in reply to my first question, "has been an inner drive after knowledge. But, to bring me any satisfaction, this knowledge must be free from obscurity and confusion. I have felt the need to make my knowledge more and more clear, more and more refined. I want knowledge that is, as far as possible, exact. That knowledge can be obtained, it seems to me, better through science than through anything else. Therefore I have pursued science."

"Has not the aesthetic aspect of science also been an incentive? Have you not felt attracted by the beauty of the scientific picture of the world?"

"But certainly. The beauty of science is one of the rewards of scientific study. Truth and beauty, in science, lie very close together. But they are not the same thing. Yet they always accompany one another."

"Would you say that one aspect is more important than the other?"

"How can one decide their relative importance?" asked the Professor, smiling. "It is like asking me which is the more important, the lock or the key."

"Since beauty is so prominent an element in science, would you say that science and the arts are akin? Could science be regarded, essentially, as a great work of art?"

"There is certainly a kinship between science and art, but, at the same time, the differences are very marked. Science is a result of the desire for knowledge. The beauty of science arises from the fact that there exists a close connection between truth and beauty. This connection is probably due to the very structure of our minds. But the primary aim of the scientific man is not beauty, but knowledge. In this he differs from the artist, whose primary concern is beauty. But, in his search for beauty, the artist can also reveal to us truth and knowledge. Thus science and art are akin, and yet they are also different."

"What do you think is the chief importance of science to mankind?"

"I put first the part it has played in making men more intelligent. The effort to create science has led men to adopt a certain method of thought. There are, *a priori*, various ways in which the mind can function. It can build up various fantasies, it can adopt various ways of reasoning. Which, of all these methods, is best adapted to dealing with reality? The development of intelligence is the development of the art of successful thinking. Science has shown men that, to be successful, a certain way of thinking is necessary. By pursuing this method one can gain real knowledge. Since science can be created only by correct thinking, the pursuit of science has aided the growth of intelligence. "Science is also important to mankind for its practical applications."

"Do you think that mankind has progressed?"

"Man has progressed in the sense that he has acquired a greater mastery of natural laws. This mastery has necessitated, as I have said, a progress in intelligence, and it has led to great material progress. For all the material advantages of our civilization can be traced, of course, to our mastery of natural laws. Both in intelligence and in material matters, mankind has progressed."

"And morally?"

"No, I do not think there has been any moral progress."

"But surely men are less cruel than they used to be. We could not have witch-burning now, for example."

"I agree that we could not have witch-burning now, but I think that what appears as greater kindliness is merely an expression of what could be called better manners. The moral character of man expresses itself in different ways in different ages. The beliefs that led to witch-burning are no longer held. Man does not, nowadays, manifest his impulses in that way. His growth and intelligence has made such things impossible. But this does not mean that he has a kinder heart. Modern man finds outlets for his impulses along different lines, but I can see no improvement in the moral character he displays. I do not believe that man has progressed morally."

"Do you think that life and consciousness are the outcome of the random action of natural laws, or do you think that they form part of some great scheme?"

"I believe that life is part of some greater life that we cannot understand. But this is not a scientific belief. It is a belief that must be justified on quite other than scientific grounds. Your question can only be answered by a fantasy."

"A fantasy?"

"A fantasy is a way of representing things to oneself in other than scientific terms. The beliefs that are expressed in a fantasy are not amenable to scientific tests. They are beliefs of a different order from beliefs that rest on scientific evidence. Your question is not one that can be decided by bringing forward scientific evidence. Nevertheless, it is a question concerning which beliefs may be held."

"How are such beliefs to be justified?"

"By their influence on character. Such beliefs cannot be sincerely held without profoundly influencing character. A man's character can be the outcome of such beliefs. And the resultant character is the justification or condemnation of the beliefs. This is the only way in which such beliefs can be judged. The scientific criteria of true and false cannot be applied to them. Moral and scientific beliefs are justified on quite different grounds."

"Do you think that consciousness can be explained in terms of matter and its laws?"

"No. I regard consciousness as fundamental. I regard matter as derivative from consciousness. We cannot get behind consciousness. Everything that we talk about, everything that we regard as existing, postulates consciousness."

In reply to another question concerning the notorious difficulties that beset modern physics, particularly in the phenomena of light, where we apparently have to use two sets of ideas that are in contradiction to one another, I found that Professor Planck considers that these difficulties illustrate the extent to which the world of science depends upon the mind. For he considers that these difficulties arise simply because we regard certain concepts as being objective realities. Thus we assume that everything that exists in nature exists in space and time. The material universe, we assume, is something that exists in space and time. When we regard certain modern scientific entities, e.g., the light-quantum, from this point of view, they seem to possess contradictory properties. Thus certain experiments show that the light-quantum is very large and other experiments show that it is very small. Planck suggests that the light-quantum is something to which the notions of spatial and temporal extension do not apply. Men must learn to regard space and time, not as objective realities to which everything must conform, but as concepts which, in this region of phenomena, must now be transcended. They are not objective realities, independent of consciousness, and perhaps none such exist.

I found, however, that he does not share the belief, held by some of the younger physicists, that nature does not form a rigidly determined system. He admits that, in the present state of research, the so-called Principle of Indeterminacy, which puts something like free-will at the basis of phenomena, is a useful scientific tool. But he regards it merely as a temporary device, and not as a discovery concerning the ultimate character of the material universe.

PROFESSOR SCHRÖDINGER

PROFESSOR SCHRÖDINGER, one of the most brilliant of the younger school of physicists, has won his reputation chiefly by his work on the theory of the atom. His work well exemplifies the tendency of modern physics to become so abstract as to be entirely non-picturable. Schrödinger himself regards this tendency as a passing phase. He thinks that the new theories will ultimately assume a picturable form, and that science will once more become "intelligible" to the layman.

"I took up mathematics and physics quite early, as part of my ordinary school course," said Professor Schrödinger. "I found that I liked these studies, and I conceived the project of going on to the technical high school in order to devote myself to the practical applications of science. But I found that I should have to learn geometrical drawing, and this prospect appalled me. So I went to the University instead, and concentrated on pure science. That really suited me much better, of course. But I must not give the impression that science alone interested me. As a matter of fact, my early desire was to be a poet. But I speedily realised that poetry was not a paying business. Science, on the other hand, offered me a career."

"What do you find to be, now, your chief interest in science?"

"The aesthetic interest. But science does not merely consist in composing beautiful theories. That would be too easy. The fact that theories have to fit the external world means that the aesthetic criterion alone is not sufficient. Science, really, is a game played according to certain rules."

"What do you consider to be the chief importance of science to mankind?"

"Well, it so happens that I have just been writing about this very point. I have come to the conclusion that the chief function of science is to give pleasure. In fact, I rank sport, art, and science together. They are all forms of play."

"How do you arrive at that conclusion?"

"By realising that sport, art, science, are merely outlets for superfluous energy. We notice that when an animal is released to some extent from the struggle for existence, it begins to play. Thus domesticated animals, which depend on us for their food, use their superfluous energy in play. When man had to some extent conquered his environment, so that his whole life was no longer a struggle for bare existence, he began to play. He invented sports, he invented the arts, and he invented science. All these things are forms of play. They exist to give man pleasure."

"But surely the pleasure given by science is experienced by very few people?"

"Yes, that is true. And it is customary to say that the importance of science for mankind in general is to be found in the practical applications of science. But I do not think this point of view is altogether correct. Undoubtedly some of the applications of science do lead to desirable results. For instance, I think it is a good thing that people should be enabled to see large parts of the earth. And I think that the facilities for transport and communication have a good side inasmuch as they bring peoples closer together. But many of our modern achievements are of no real value at all. I recently spent some time in the heart of the country, remote from all modern conveniences. I did not find that the absence of these conveniences made me unhappy. I believe that we do not really want many of the things that science has given us. Fast motor cars, the radio, and so on, are all things that we can do without perfectly well. The real fun of such things is in inventing them and making them work. It is the joy of construction and of solving a problem. It is a great pleasure to feel that we can actually dominate nature so far as to bring these extraordinary machines into existence. We gain a sense of power and have delight in our own ingenuity. But, having got the things, we do not really gain any benefits by using them. We use them simply because we have got them. Suppose, for instance, that we invent a ship that will go to America in twenty-four hours. We would be very pleased at having invented such a ship. The achievement would give us great pleasure. But who really wants to go to America in twenty-four hours? Merchants may imagine that they want to rush about the world at great speeds, but they are not a bit the happier for it. The so-called 'advances' of civilisation are not, to my mind, benefits at all, except for the intellectual pleasure they give."

"When you said just now that science is a game, a form of play, did you mean that it is a game in the sense that chess is a game? If so, how is it that science gives us information about reality, whereas chess does not?"

"Well, chess is a very limited game." Professor Schrödinger then proceeded to calculate the total number of combinations possible in chess. The result was curious and interesting, but would hardly enlighten the non-arithmetical reader. "Now in science," the Professor went on, "the number of combinations is infinite. It is not surprising that some of them should coincide with the way phenomena actually happen."

"I'm afraid the point is not yet clear to me," I replied. "I understand that somebody has invented a chessboard with more squares and pieces. This process could be continued. But, however long it went on and however many games were played, no light would be thrown on the nature of reality."

The Professor smiled. "Yes, I'm afraid that science cannot be merely a game," he replied. "As a matter of fact, I think that the material universe and consciousness are made out of the same stuff. It is not, to me, a matter for great surprise that man should be able to find out the laws according to which nature works. We cannot speak of nature as something separate from mind. The nature we talk about is the nature that exists for our minds; we cannot possibly know of any other."

"Then what would you think of Eddington's remark that nature may finally turn out to be irrational?"

"That is altogether unthinkable," said Schrödinger with vivacity. "In fact," he said, smiling, "even if nature really *is* irrational, we could never, never believe it. Science cannot possibly be given up."

"Do you think that mankind has progressed?"

"I do not believe that the individual man has progressed morally. But I think that the mass moral consciousness is higher.

"Communities know more of one another; they are

less isolated. And this leads to a greater mutual sympathy. Inter-community feeling is certainly less ruthless than it was, but the individual member of any community has not improved. On the other hand, there has been, I think, an intellectual development."

"Do you think that life on this planet is a result of some sort of accident, or do you think it is part of some great scheme?"

"Life, as we know it, certainly seems to be dependent on rather special physical conditions. If one studies the Periodic Table of the Elements, for example, one finds that the element carbon seems to possess quite unusual properties. These properties are peculiarly fitted for building up organic bodies. Supposing carbon did not exist on this planet, would life be able to appear? It seems to be unlikely, although, of course, there may be forms of life of which we know nothing. But all life on this planet is dependent on carbon, and carbon alone seems to have just the extraordinary properties that are necessary. It might well be, therefore, that life is the result of an accident or coincidence. This planet happens to have had just the right chemical substance, and the right physical conditions of temperature and so on, to make life possible. But I do not think it at all likely that life is confined to this planet. To suppose so would seem to me against all the probabilities. On any scientific theory of the origin of planets there must be a large number of them scattered through the material universe. And the material substances with which we are familiar seem to be everywhere. Even on the doctrine of pure chance, therefore, I should consider it most unlikely that life exists only on this planet."

"But all activity in the universe must, it appears,

some day come to an end. When that happens there will be no life anywhere in the universe. Will life then have been an episode of no permanent significance?"

"There can be no significance without life. Even if life here be the only life in the universe, then that life is the justification, the focus, of the whole thing."

"But if it comes to an end?"

"I am no more frightened by time than I am by space," said Schrödinger, smiling. "Life here is confined to a small space in the universe. It may also be confined to a small time. But if this life is the only life, then the whole meaning of the universe, throughout its extent and throughout its history, is to be found here. But although I think that life may be the result of an accident, I do not think that of consciousness. Consciousness cannot be accounted for in physical terms. For consciousness is absolutely fundamental. It cannot be accounted for in terms of anything else."

PRINCE DE BROGLIE

"I was brought up in an atmosphere of science," said the Prince de Broglie in reply to my question as to how he came to take up science. "My brother was a mature man of science while I was still a youth. I suppose that his example turned my attention to the subject. And then I discovered that I had a natural taste for it. I went on with science because I found that the study gave me great pleasure."

"Would you describe that pleasure as aesthetic or as the gratification of a desire for knowledge?"

"I really cannot say. I suppose that truth and aesthetics, in science, can be separated, theoretically. But when it comes to practice, when it comes to one's own motives in pursuing science, I find it impossible to make the distinction. I cannot say which most attracts me in a scientific theory, its truth or its beauty. I do not know whether one can exist without the other. So that if you ask me which of these has most influenced me I am afraid I cannot tell you."

"What would you say is the chief importance of science for mankind?"

"I do not think that it has any influence on conduct. I do not believe that scientific knowledge influences a man's moral character at all. The reason why science is studied is because that study gives pleasure—aesthetic pleasure, if you like—to scientific men."

"But the pleasures of scientific study can be experienced by very few people."

"Yes, just a few specialists."

"Then why should mankind in general value science?"

"Well, it so happens that science issues in certain practical applications. These applications are of benefit to mankind as a whole. That is what the ordinary man gets out of science, and it is a sufficiently good reason for him to support it. But science is not valued by scientific men for its practical applications. Science is valued by the public on quite different grounds from those on which scientific men value it."

"Do you think that life is a fortuitous happening in the universe?"

"I can hardly believe that life is fortuitous. In fact, I have a strong impression that life cannot have arisen fortuitously."

"Then it must be part of a scheme?"

"Yes."

"Is it possible, do you think, to know anything about the scheme?"

"It may be possible. But such knowledge could not be gained by scientific means. If such knowledge is obtainable it must be knowledge of a different kind from scientific knowledge. I do not know what sort of knowledge it could be; but I would not say that such knowledge is impossible."

"Do you think that art communicates knowledge?"

"I think that art gives us information about our feelings. I do not think that it gives us any other sort of knowledge. But such knowledge is perfectly real knowledge. It is also knowledge of a quite different kind from scientific knowledge. For nothing can be known about a state of feeling by scientific means.

Science could possibly detect the physical phenomena that accompany feelings, but the state of feeling itself could not be recorded on any scientific instrument. Yet we know that we feel. That is indisputable. It is knowledge quite as real as scientific knowledge."

"And you think that art is concerned with such knowledge?"

"Yes, art communicates knowledge about feelings. Art and science perform very different functions, since they deal with quite different kinds of knowledge. If one wished to find a resemblance between science and art, one could find it only in the fact that science is also beautiful. Otherwise they are quite separate."

"Do you think that mankind has progressed and is progressing?"

"I think that we must say that material progress has taken place. But if that is what is meant by progress it is quite possible that progress will not continue. It is doubtful whether material improvements can go on indefinitely. All such improvements consist in utilising the forces of nature, which obey certain laws. These laws cannot be superseded, and they set a limit to what is possible. And, even before this limit is reached, we may find that material progress reaches its maximum from other considerations. If progress is made a matter of merely material improvements, then it seems likely that the race cannot progress for ever."

"Do you think that man has progressed intellectually?"

"Yes."

"And morally?"

"That is more doubtful. I think that the individual man has progressed morally in certain respects. I think that he is less cruel, for example. But I cannot see that nations are less cruel. Mass morality is, at present, on a lower level than individual morality. When it is a case of nation against nation, I can see no moral improvement compared with former times. So that, although the individual is less cruel, it is difficult to say, without qualification, that mankind has progressed morally."

"Do you think that the present social system, with its rewards and discouragements, tends to produce the best type of man?"

The Prince smiled. "That, I am afraid, is a matter about which I have no opinion," he said.

"Do you think that anything of a man's personality survives his bodily death?"

"It is purely a matter of evidence, and to my mind the evidence is not sufficient to justify one in believing in survival. I would say that there is *no* evidence of survival."

"Heisenberg's Principle of Indeterminacy (the Prince brightened perceptibly) is, I understand, a statement to the effect that our scientific measurements cannot reveal to us a perfectly deterministic system in nature. He states that it is impossible for us to predict accurately, from the present state of affairs, what the future state of affairs will be. What, in your opinion, is the status of this principle? Is it merely a statement of our temporary ignorance, or is it to be taken as a discovery that nature does not form a strictly determined system?"

"I regard the Principle of Indeterminacy as fundamental. It is not to be considered merely as a useful device at the present stage of science; that is to say, a device that may in future be superseded. It expresses a fundamental characteristic of the universe. The old scientific outlook, which assumed that nature forms a perfectly determined scheme, must be given up."

"Do you think that consciousness can be explained in terms of matter?"

"No. I do not see how consciousness can be derived from material things."

"Do you think that matter exists independently of consciousness?"

"I regard consciousness and matter as different aspects of one thing. There is one substance out of which both consciousness and matter are built. The aspect of this substance that we examine by scientific methods is what we call matter. The other aspect of which we obtain knowledge, not scientifically, but directly, is what we call consciousness."

PROFESSOR LEVY

"My chief personal interest in doing scientific work," said Professor Levy, "arises from the pleasure I obtain in discovering truth. This is where I find science more attractive than any other activity. It is much more satisfactory than philosophy in this respect for the reason that science is much more definite in its conclusions. Scientific questions have to be put precisely in order that definite answers may be furnished. Philosophical questions, it seems to me, are seldom, if ever, so stated that a decisive answer can be forthcoming at all."

"But are not scientific questions always being given different answers? Is it not true that science is continually changing?"

"The answers change because the scientific environment of the questions change. This change is a change in the environment of scientific knowledge and is produced by the forward march of the scientific movement itself. But granted this change there is a constantly increasing residuum which remains pretty constant, remaining true whatever happens. In philosophy this does not appear to be the case. Philosophers simply agree to differ apparently. Science depends absolutely on the fact that at each stage such differences must be resolved. But although I should say that its truth-finding value in this sense is the great attraction that science now has for me, my earlier reactions were somewhat different. I was fascinated to begin with by the sheer cogency of a mathematical argument. The purity and definiteness of this reasoning had an extraordinary attraction for me. Later on I was amazed to discover that these purely abstract exercises could be applied to the actual real solid world."

"And would you describe this interest as aesthetic?"

"Undoubtedly, for surely with human beings there can be no intellectual exercise that is not accompanied with an emotional reaction and a sense of pleasurable appreciation. There is real beauty, for example, in a closely argued and well balanced mathematical discourse. To the individual the aesthetic interest in science is very marked, and although the individual scientist is a unit in a forward movement, he is essentially an artist. In the actual pursuit of scientific research mere observation and reasoning is not alone involved. He guesses or senses in advance, scrambling slowly in the rear with his apparatus or his reasoning. Nevertheless, in spite of many personal similarities between its adherents, science is not an art. They are two different manifestations or aspects of society. They perform different functions, and their criteria of what may or may not be accepted as accredited works in their respective fields are totally different."

"Do you think that life is purposeless or part of some great scheme?"

"What can you mean by purpose? It seems to me that purpose is a notion that can only be applied by an individual to his acts. An intelligible meaning to purpose in any other sense could be forthcoming only when we had some public method of recognising its existence. In the other sense of course there is purpose in the universe since man is part of it. We must always remember that nothing exists in the universe independently, as an isolate so to speak, including man himself. Science is particularly interested in the circumstances that expose apparent permanencies like objects and certain regular recurrencies, like the regular rising and setting of the sun. That is why it concerns itself so much with space, time and matter, as if they were separately existing entities. But these things have actually been drawn from their environments, and to talk of them as if they formed totally isolated systems is to denature them. But this process of isolation is inherent in scientific method. We account for the behaviour of the isolated object in its environment by fixing properties to the object, such as attractive forces for example. We abstract our notions of atoms and electrons in turn by this process from the real world, trying to fix permanent properties on to them to account for their continually varying behaviour. It may ultimately prove to be impossible to proceed further in this way, in which case science will require to develop a new technique of explanation. I suggest that some of our modern theoretical difficulties arise in this way. As we isolate atoms and electrons in thought from the environment in what we call matter, and endeavour to describe them in the comparatively simple way we do, we are actually impoverishing them in the process and then, strangely enough, we seem surprised to find that we cannot build up the actual concrete world from these denatured elements. Science in this sense at present gives a partial view of the world. As a movement it can much more readily be considered as isolated from its individual adherents than, say, art. Purpose is not a possible scientific concept; it may be an artistic one."

"Do you think that the mystical view of things may possibly be justified?"

"If I understand correctly what you are suggesting by mystical, the question implies the existence of some kind of criterion for the acceptance of a statement as a truth, even if it has been derived by some mystical process. Science is of course concerned as much with the process of arriving at a truth as with the truth itself."

"What are the criteria you would demand in this case?"

"They are the same as I would apply to science. There any new statement must not diverge too drastically from the scientific tradition as it has been developed up till now, and the statement must be capable of verification by some process that can be followed by other members of the scientific movement from definite instructions provided. Thus if what you call mysticism fulfils these conditions it may be a legitimate method of approach to what is called scientific knowledge. If not it is dealing with a different matter and the word 'justified' in your question conveys nothing to me."

"Do you think that mankind has progressed?"

"The question is indefinite, but I certainly think that man has it now in his power to establish a greater degree of control over the material forces of nature than in the past."

"And moral progress?"

"I should be inclined to say so, yes. For moral progress is I suspect largely conditioned by material progress. In many ways individuals are much less cruel, for example, than they were formerly, but on the other hand they are also more sensitive to cruelty. They are simply two aspects of the same form of moral progress, but they imply that we may not recognise at once that we have become less cruel. Of course we still tolerate an extraordinary degree of corporate cruelty as a community. The difficulty is I think that moral progress drags along in the wake of material progress, sometimes far in the wake, with the result that, as a community, we are simply muddling along, exercising a much greater corporate cruelty than any of us individually would dream of doing."

"What do you think of the Greek ideal of the perfectly balanced life?"

"Well, it is one form of communal development we may see, but for success it implies the existence of a class of specialist denied this balanced life or not desiring it, to provide the wherewithal to preserve the balance and to raise its level."

"What do you think of the present social system of rewards and discouragements?"

"Well, we haven't tried any other system. But I see not the faintest reason to suppose that a scientifically designed system aiming to secure maximum communal efficiency would be even approximately like the present absurd and vicious one."

"What should be the criterion of rewards for a man's work?"

"I cannot see any simple one. All work is so interlocked that it is impossible to discuss any single contribution as if it were isolated. Most of our major public needs can be supplied by public services like highways and street lighting. Our private need would have to be met in some other way. In any case I do not see, apart from exceptional individuals, that the system of rewards should bear any simple relation to the nature of the work performed. That is simply a social habit we have got into. Capacity for digestion is also a factor to be considered."

"Then what do you think of Shaw's idea for an equal wage for everybody?"

"I think that solution is too flat."

"Do you regard consciousness as fundamental in the universe?"

"I think that question illustrates our habit, that I mentioned before, of constructing isolated systems. There are conscious beings in the universe, conscious of their environment and demonstrating that consciousness through interaction with their environment. You cannot therefore separate one or the other out and say this one is more fundamental than that one. It is false isolation. But you or I experience our consciousnesses in each our own way, and reacting to the environment tend to imagine that each such form of consciousness is fundamental and the world constructed on it as a basis. So far is this from being established that I cannot even compare mine with yours, and if I refer to mine as consciousness I have no test to apply to verify that I am not committing a gross fallacy in also calling yours by the same name. It seems to me that we cannot approach the matter in that way at all. We have no justification for making such a hard and fast isolation. What we will call your consciousness was born in time and will I suppose die. It has a history and it has unfolded in the universe. It exists in the universe. The universe does not exist in it as I can testify."

"But do you believe then that there is an objective something quite independent of the mind?"

"Of my mind, yes, but not completely independent, because your mind and mine are parts of it. No more than the tree exists independent of the leaves. If however you mean, does the world go out of existence when you die? Of course not. Even after I die I suppose there will still be a sensible meaning to the phrase, 'the universe exists,' but I shall not appreciate it."

MR. H. G. WELLS

(*This interview is the author's condensed account of his recollection of a long and desultory conversation that was pursued at different places and times. It is presented in the form of consecutive questions and answer merely in order to make it uniform with the other interviews.*)

MR. H. G. WELLS is of the opinion that his career has resulted from his inability to pack parcels. "From the age of thirteen to the age of fifteen and a half," he said, "I quite honestly tried to be a draper's assistant. My discovery that I could not pack parcels led me to seek another career. I became a schoolmaster. If it had not been for that inability I think I should still be a second-rate draper's assistant."

"You are serious?"

"Well, I always had a certain innate pugnacity. As a schoolmaster, for instance, I refused to teach the scriptures."

"When, finally, you began to write, what was the chief interest of writing to you?"

"The delight of finding the apt phrase. To say a thing vividly and exactly seemed to be the real fun of writing. And then, gradually, the desire grew in me to express a point of view. This desire became much stronger after the war. The war stopped all my playing. I used to be fond of playing at a war game, you know—I've written a little book about it—with Masterman and

Cecil Chesterton and others. But I've never once played that game since 1914. How can one play games in a world where Mussolini and Al Capone are facts? I've come to realise that they are facts: they are not flowers of some kind. As a result, I think that even an imperfectly written statement which helps things forward is more valuable than a perfect work of art. It is better to be tenth rate in this line than to be a first-rate artist. To concentrate on being an artist, in the present state of affairs, is a waste of opportunities. There are plenty of people who would be first-class bridge players, but they have something better to do. That is how I have come to look at art. Since the war I have had a continually intensified sense of an impending world collapse. I mean a complete collapse, financial, and every other way. And I believe that the only thing that can save us is coherent planning instead of incoherent experimenting."

"Do you believe that there is a universal scheme of which our lives form a part?"

"If there is a scheme, it is altogether outside our consciousness. We live in a world where space has three dimensions and time is a reality. We have to think of everything in these terms. But I think it is also possible that the universe is static and four-dimensional."

"How do you reconcile these two points of view?"

"I don't find it necessary to reconcile them. The drama of life may be like a film that is being run through the machine. On the film everything already exists. If we are thinking of the static film, everything is already there, and there is no drama, for there is no succession of incidents in time. But we cannot survey the film except bit by bit, and it is the succession that produces the drama. This is analogous, it seems to me, to the relation between life and the four-dimensional static reality."

"Do you think it possible, in any way, to make direct contact with this extra-human reality?"

"No. I think that all our feeling and thinking is necessarily limited by human values. I do not believe that mystical religious meditation is anything more than a looking back on experience and trying to make it coherent. When, in some of my books, I have pictured men retiring to lonely places to meditate in solitude it is always this kind of meditation that I have had in mind. I do not believe that religious meditation is a search for something new. It is not a method of making contact with some extra-human reality. In fact, I do not believe that a specific religious instinct or faculty, in that sense, exists. Man is entirely limited to thoughts and aspirations which are concerned with human values—with the life and development of the human race. The mind has no power to transcend these limitations."

"Then do you think that the meaning of life is to be found in the future of the human race? Would you, for instance, find the justification of suffering in the future happiness of mankind?"

"I know of no solution of the problem of suffering. But I certainly would not look to a solution in the future happiness of man. I must go back to the four-dimensional view. Although the justification of the present is not to be found in the future, yet it may be that the whole justifies its parts. The film, as a whole, may hang perfectly together. It is not a question of good bits, making up for bad bits, although, if you take any normal life, I think you'll find that the happiness outweighs the suffering."

"Nevertheless, there are cases, such as——"

"Yes, I know. I don't really think that suffering can be accounted for in that way. Why should a baby scream for the first few days after it is brought into the world? You have the whole problem of suffering there. It seems to me unanswerable."

"Do you think that anything of a man survives his bodily death?"

"I do not believe at all in the survival of the individual. A man can be said to survive his death only to the extent to which he has made a contribution to the mind of the race."

"Then if the human race comes to an end that will be the finish of the whole thing?"

"Yes."

"Do you believe, then, that the material universe is quite independent of consciousness, and would persist in the absence of consciousness?"

"I think that the material universe is an objective reality. Nevertheless, I think that consciousness, in some form, was always present in the universe. I do not believe that it suddenly appeared out of nothing. But one must be careful in saying this. Consciousness, as we know it, arises from inhibited reflexes. It could not exist in the absence of physiological machinery. But some primitive form of it must always have existed. Consciousness is a developing thing, and it must have come from some rudimentary origin. All our difficulties about these questions come from the fact that consciousness is still imperfectly developed. Our minds can deal pretty adequately with things in our immediate neighbourhood—this chair, or that table, for instance. But when we come to such things as space and time the inadequacy of our minds is very evident. Many of these problems are due, I believe, to the imperfections of the instrument we use in dealing with them—that is, our consciousness. Our minds were developed to deal with practical problems having a bearing on the question of survival. Other matters are not really within our range. That is why I think that philosophy and theology will ultimately be given up. They will be replaced by science, which is a legitimate field of inquiry for our essentially practical minds."

"Yet science, of recent years, seems to be becoming more and more metaphysical."

"Perhaps it is. But I am not in sympathy with that movement. In fact, I believe that scientific men discuss philosophy only in moments of weakness."

"Do you think that, in our present society, the system of rewards is adapted to encourage the best in men?"

"I think that our present systems of incentives and discouragements are so ill-chosen that, if they are not changed, our present social system will not even survive. Our present system contains elements within it which, if they are not counteracted, will lead to its destruction. The most urgent need at the present time is the need for the reconstruction of our whole State of society. But the task is so enormous that, I confess, one quails before it."

"Do you believe that mankind has progressed and is progressing?"

"There seems to be different notions as to what constitutes progress. But from my point of view mankind has progressed. Men have greatly increased their range of movement and of communication. They have also greatly increased their power over Nature. Also, they live longer lives, and their sensibilities have increased. Life is fuller and more varied than it used to be. All this, to my mind, constitutes progress, and if man continues to advance in these directions I shall say that he is progressing."

"What do you think of the Greek ideal of the perfectly balanced life?"

"If we regard it as a statement of a man's potentialities it is sensible enough. A man could climb the Himalayas, or travel in Japan, or have a love affair with an African princess, or work in a metallurgical laboratory, or write a book, or be a coal-miner. But he cannot do all these things at once. In practice, he will have to be content with one or two of these activities. One mode of life rules out the other modes of life. The Greek ideal, therefore, as a practical ideal, is merely silly."

"You do not think, therefore, that exclusive devotion to one thing—for example, Isaac Newton's complete devotion to science—is undesirable?"

"No. I should call Newton's a good life. But it was an abnormal good life. It was an extreme case. And I should like to say, by the way, that I don't believe that the Greeks, or anybody else, ever lived in accordance with the so-called Greek ideal. I believe that ideal is founded merely on a few selected quotations from Greek literature. It has been put together by a few scholars. The Greeks never held any such ideal. I think that what people really want to do is to make a contribution to the general human stock. I think this explains all sorts of silly and showy exploits which seem to be undertaken merely to secure notoriety for their authors. I think that something better than mere vanity is involved, at bottom. They are attempts, even if they be silly and misguided attempts, to make a contribution."

ON PROGRESS

BEFORE we can answer the question, "Has mankind progressed?" we must know, of course, what we mean by progress. And any answer we give will be very largely conditioned by the spirit of the age in which we live. In discussing questions of morality, in particular, our judgments will be influenced by the moral standards current in our time. Virtues vary in importance from age to age. They depend very largely upon the practical conditions of life. The virtue of physical courage, for instance, is probably not as highly esteemed to-day as it would have been by a robber baron of the Middle Ages. Our judgments of moral progress, we must remember, are exceptionally likely to be based on merely local considerations.

Progress, it is evident, is of three main kinds—material, moral and intellectual. So far as our material civilization is concerned, it is obvious enough that mankind has progressed. In the two great and essential activities of transport and communication (under which latter head we may rank the cinema and the wireless), the world is incomparably better off than it has ever been before. That is obvious. But can it be maintained that such increased facilities are an unmixed blessing? There are some writers who profess to find much that is undesirable in these modern achievements. Rapid transit and communication, the wireless and the cinema have, according to these writers, largely destroyed individuality. They have made life more uniform and more banal. There is much to be said for this point of view, but the state of affairs it deplores seems to be due to the fact that the population of the civilized world has greatly increased, and that the average human being is now much more prominent than he ever was before. It is probably not true that the ordinary man is less moral or less intelligent than he was in the past. In fact, he is probably more intelligent, at any rate. But it is only recently that his tastes and desires have claimed so much attention. And his immense numerical preponderance enables him to play the dominating role. It is probable, for instance, that the average quality of the literature published in England to-day is lower than it would be in a country containing only an educated and leisured class and an illiterate peasantry. We may take it that the educated class would not read books of more than a certain degree of imbecility. In England to-day, where books are produced for every level of education and intelligence, the average quality is necessarily lower. But this is no evidence of deterioration.

It is generally agreed that there is no evidence that the human mind has ever reached a higher level than it reached in ancient Athens. But although the actual mental capacity and energy of the human mind may not have increased it may nevertheless be true that it is now employed in a more effective manner. Professor Max Planck has put forward the interesting idea that the adoption of the scientific method of thought has led to a real increase of intelligence. For intelligence may be regarded, in one aspect at least, as an instrument for ensuring successful adaptation between man and the universe. For the efficiency of this instrument the method of thought is quite as important as the energy expended. The analogical reasoning current in the Middle Ages, and now current in certain schools of psycho-analysis, is a less efficient method of thought than is the scientific method. Immense ingenuity, brilliant fancy, and great mental energy may be displayed, but the method employed does not enable the thinker to fulfil his purpose, which is to get at the truth. The adoption of the scientific method, by enabling the intellect to function more efficiently, has increased intelligence. It is highly probable that a thinker to-day actually gets through a greater quantity of successful thinking than would have been possible to him at any previous period of history. And if we suppose that the best modern minds, amongst those employing the scientific method, are fully comparable, in native capacity, with the best minds of antiquity, then we may say that the human race has reached a higher level of intelligence to-day than ever before.

Just as it may be maintained that the average art, literature, architecture and so on of to-day is lower than it has been in the past, so it may be asserted that the average intelligence is lower. Those who believe that we are suffering from a rapid multiplication of the lower human stocks think that this lower average is due to an actual inferiority in the quality of the race. But, here again, we must remember that whole sections of the community have become vocal that were never vocal before. There is no reason to suppose that, at any former time, they would have demanded anything better than they demand to-day. The difference is that their demands are now supplied. The modern popular press, for example, is certainly, in some ways, a disconcerting phenomenon, and it is true that it could not have existed a hundred years ago. But it could not have existed for the simple reason that its potential readers could not read.

It is probable that the average intelligence is higher to-day than it has ever been. Practically every human being in every civilized community has access to cheap reading matter and a large proportion of them experience such other stimulating influences as the cinema, the theatre, etc. Although the stimulus afforded by these influences may be of a relatively low grade, it is nevertheless a stimulus which, on this scale, has never been known before. And stimulus is necessary to the development of intelligence. Against this we may put the fact that, with the immense spread of industrialism most men are engaged in daily tasks of a very uniform and monotonous character. The modern working man, compared with the old craftsman, has practically no demands made upon his intelligence. His work, in perhaps the majority of cases, does actually deaden intelligence. But we may doubt whether the deadening effect of his toil is not more than compensated by the excitements of his leisure. It is probable that the life of the ordinary man, to-day, is less boring than it has ever been. It is probable, therefore, that the level of ordinary intelligence has risen.

There seems to be considerable diversity of opinion concerning the question of man's moral progress. The conclusion we arrive at seems to depend, for many people, chiefly on whether we suppose mankind to have become less cruel. It is this characteristic, more than any other, that influences our judgment. An age which permits, for example, witch-burning is, we are convinced, less morally developed than one which does not, to whatever extent it may have excelled in other virtues. If, therefore, we are convinced that men have grown more kindly, we shall assert that they have progressed.

It seems possible for some people to doubt whether mankind in general has grown less cruel. Professor Max Planck thinks that there has been no change in this respect. The fact that we do not burn witches now merely indicates, he thinks, that we have different manners, not different morals. The burning of witches was concerned with a certain system of beliefs; we no longer hold those beliefs, and therefore we no longer find it necessary to burn witches. But the impulses that found their satisfaction in witch-burning have not ceased to exist; they have merely found different channels of expression. It might be difficult to refute this argument directly, but we can make it less probable by pointing to advances which seem to testify to a positive growth in human kindliness, and not merely to the diversion of certain impulses into other channels. We may instance such facts as that executions no longer take place in public, the decline in popularity of bloodsports, the formation of the societies for the prevention of cruelty to children and animals, the fact that certain barbarous punishments are no longer inflicted on criminals, the steadily increasing movement towards prison reform, the adoption of more humane methods in the slaughter house. All these movements testify to one thing —the growth of humaneness. It might be pointed out that these advances have been brought about, as in fact they have, by the persistent efforts of a small minority, and that they indicate nothing whatever concerning the moral condition of the mass of the people. But we can hardly doubt that the majority of these measures are now secure of general approval, and that any attempt to introduce the earlier outlook on these matters would meet with a vigorous popular resistance.

There remains Sir Josiah Stamp's question as to whether humanitarianism is desirable. Would it not be better in the long run, biologically, if men became hard and unsympathetic? This question is merely inviting us, of course, to substitute one set of values for another. It may be, for instance, that a hard and unsympathetic race of men, basing all their actions on self-interest, would reach a greater degree of efficiency in certain directions, or perhaps stand a greater chance of survival, than would otherwise be possible. But we could not consider this an improvement unless we regarded efficiency or survival as so desirable an end that love and kindness might well be sacrificed for it. With our present outlook this conclusion would seem to be impossible, and therefore the question is, in a sense, unreal. Nevertheless, such a state of affairs may actually come about. It may be that human nature is so plastic that a few eugenists, with unlimited power, might be able to produce a race of human tigers. And if all our moral values are relative, if it be indeed true that man makes God in his own image, then doubtless the human tigers would consider themselves superior to the present kind of man. But so, presumably, would any other race that the eugenists might produce. We have to judge such claims to superiority on the basis of our present scale of values, and this remains true whether or not these values are absolute. But if our values are absolute we can definitely say that the human tigers would not be an improvement. If our values are not absolute, then the question is meaningless, since, in that case, nothing is either good or bad, but thinking makes it so.

Nevertheless, the question brings into prominence the important fact that progress in certain directions is incompatible with progress in others. If, for instance, our ideal is to make man a perfect member of society, then we cannot also make him a perfect individual. Most modern communities, particularly those of Russia and the United States, tend to produce a standardized man, relatively lacking in individuality but able, for that very reason, to be a more efficient member of society. It is possible that this process is destined to go far. Bertrand Russell* has envisaged the creation of a world-state, created deliberately with a certain structure in order to fulfil certain purposes. Scientific technique, he thinks, makes such a deliberate creation possible. Assuming a sufficient increase in biological and psychological knowledge the rulers of such a state could realise any ideal they set before themselves. Mr. Russell pictures a state whose ideal is power, and shows how completely insignificant love and art would become in such a state. Men would no longer be individuals, ends in themselves, but instruments. A more picturesque version of this possibility is given in Wells's *First Men in the Moon*. It will be remembered that the members of that highly scientific community had their bodies, as well as their minds, formed and trained for the particular kind of work allotted to them.

These speculations regarding man's possible future

* "The Scientific Outlook."

all assume that man, as a biological organism, is extremely malleable, and this assumption far out-runs the actual scientific evidence. The experimental results hitherto obtained would have to be greatly extended before such an assumption became probable. It is usually found, in science, that a practical advance in any particular direction cannot be continued indefinitely; new factors come into play, and the process reaches a natural limitation. Thus aeroplane speeds cannot, as many newspaper writers seem to think, increase indefinitely. A limit is set to the possible speed by certain properties of the air. These properties dominate the whole problem at certain speeds; although they may be ignored at lower speeds. We are probably greatly over-simplifying the problem if we assume that the new physiology of the ductless glands, combined with a more perfect technique of propaganda, will enable us to modify human nature indefinitely. Speculations based on such an assumption are accordingly, in the present state of our knowledge, somewhat idle.

Besides assuming a scientific technique which does not, and probably never will, exist the doctrine of the infinite malleability of man also assumes, of course, that man is a completely random outcome of a random evolutionary process. For if we suppose that there is some kind of directive force in the universe, if we assume, in Lloyd Morgan's words, that evolution "is from first to last a revelation and manifestation of that which I speak of as Divine Purpose," then we cannot suppose, of course, that man's future development may take *any* direction. It must be, presumably, in accordance with the Divine Purpose. In view, however, of the remarkable ambiguity, or else relative powerless-

ON PROGRESS

ness, of the Divine Purpose, which permits all the suffering as well as all the beauty of the world, this fact is of very little help in prophesying man's future development.

Besides asking whether man has progressed morally, intellectually, and materially, we may also ask whether he has increased in sensibility. Increase in sensibility is one of the most obvious characteristics of the upward march of evolution, and if we decide that man has increased in sensibility we shall say that he has progressed.

If we compare the conditions of modern life with those of past ages we shall find it natural to suppose that sensibility has increased. The stimuli, emotional and intellectual, afforded by modern life, are surely more numerous and varied than life has ever offered before. At the same time they would appear to issue in less intense reactions. The fact that we no longer produce great works of art is perhaps an indication of that. There is something anæmic, it must be admitted, about nearly all modern productions. There is no longer that intensity of creative energy that produced Gothic Cathedrals or the tremendous works of the Renaissance. But we cover a wider field. Our art may be small, but it is extraordinarily various. Innumerable subtleties of emotion and perception have been expressed in our time which were never expressed before. And, in the mathematical sciences in particular, and even in philosophy, man has thought new thoughts, has discovered new possibilities of the mind. The intellectual life of our time is more variously peopled than it was even in the greatest creative periods of history. We may lack their energy, but we have much more than their subtlety. The general sensibility has increased. We have an obvious instance of this in the modern attitude towards sexual love. Compared with the old patriarchal attitude, or with the attitude of the Middle Ages, or even with the attitude of the eighteenth century, we see how much more complex and refined this emotion has become. Doubtless sociological changes have been partly responsible for this change of outlook, but in part it seems to be due to a genuine increase in sensibility. The characteristics of modern life foster such an increase. The mere existence of such unprecedented things as wireless, aeroplanes, motor-cars, steam locomotives, etc., expands the imagination. The facilities for cheap and rapid travel have greatly added to the ordinary man's experiences. Access to the art and thought of the whole world, past as well as present, is now easier than ever. The modern man, particularly the ordinary man, lives in an unprecedentedly rich and complex world.

We may conclude that, for the majority of civilized mankind, there has been a real moral and intellectual progress, an increase of sensibility and, of course, a great improvement in material conditions. Life is better worth living to-day, for the average man, than at any previous period in history.

www.ingramcontent.com/pod-product-compliance
Lightning Source LLC
Chambersburg PA
CBHW020331170426
43200CB00006B/349